4.00

courage
to pray

WILLIAM C. BROWNSON

D1564032

BAKER BOOK HOUSE

Grand Rapids, Michigan 49516

To
Him who loves us
and has freed us
from our sins
by his blood
and made us
a kingdom of priests
to his God and Father

Contents

Acknowledgments

I find much joy in acknowledging those who have helped to make this book possible. The Board of Directors of WORDS OF HOPE gave me a partial study leave for this purpose during the last quarter of 1987. The members of the WORDS OF HOPE staff were most understanding and cooperative throughout the project. I owe special thanks to Sue Van Otteren for typing several revisions of the manuscript, always with care and skill.

My wife, Helen, has constantly encouraged me to keep going, as have our sons Dave, Jim, and Jon, each of whom has read the manuscript and offered suggestions. Several good friends, Richard Lovelace, Malcolm Brown, and Ken and Marilyn Armstrong, have done the same.

These are among a larger company who have taught me much, who have prayed for me and with me, to whom I owe a great deal. For all of them I offer thanks to God, by whose grace we live and love and learn to pray.

Introduction

The aim of this book is to encourage you to pray. Real praying isn't easy. Sometimes it can be agonizingly difficult. All of us need wisdom to pray rightly, discipline to structure our efforts, strength to rouse ourselves for the task. But perhaps most of all, we need courage to keep at it.

Jesus once told his friends a parable for this purpose: "that they ought always to pray and not lose heart" (Luke 18:1). He knew how vulnerable we are to discouragement. When our cries for help don't seem to be heard, when vexing problems go unresolved, when pain lingers and pressures build, we are often tempted to lose heart. *What's the use?* we wonder. *Does it do any good to pray?* We need then to be somehow nerved and braced if we're to go on praying. We need to have our spirits lifted, our hearts refreshed.

Does it help to be urged to pray? Not much—not when we're down. We know already that we *should* pray. That's not our problem. But right then the duty—the obligation—seems more than we can manage.

Even the good example of others doesn't always inspire us. Accounts of another believer's heroic praying may leave us paralyzed with feelings of inadequacy—even of guilt. They succeed; we fail. They persevere in prayer; we don't. They are spiritual giants; we seem like pygmies. So run our gloomy thoughts when we've lost the heart to pray.

If that sounds like firsthand testimony, it is. I've been there. I've felt both discouraged over my weakness in prayer and self-condemned at my neglect of it. And I can remember many times when reading about the prayer habits of famous saints has both moved me to want what they had, and left me wistful, or even depressed.

It seems that many books on prayer *exhort* us better than they *enable* us. They give us reasons to pray. They show us why it is worthwhile. They offer techniques. And, if our hearts are already hungry, we find something of profit in almost all of them. But they often do not kindle faith. They do not inspire courage. They don't leave us saying, "Hey, I think I can *do* that! I believe I *can* learn to pray!"

It's possible, of course, that *this* book won't do that for you, either—but I hope it will. I'm excited because I believe it can help. The things I want to share have been so powerfully encouraging to me that those old feelings I had of frustration and defeat seldom reappear. I'm encouraged about the place prayer is gaining in my life now. It's not the sense that I've "arrived" or "attained" something, but I find myself more eager to pray than I used to be, more frequently interested in praying, more hopeful about the results. Something is happening in me so that I *want* increasingly to pray. I seem to have more heart for it than I've had before.

I thank God for that. I know it must be *his* doing. There are probably factors at work in it that I don't understand fully, but I have no doubt about what the major dynamics are. I'm realizing more and more fully that all real praying begins with him. Before it ever becomes our duty, it is first his *gift*.

As that increasingly dawns on me, I'm seeing prayer also as a *calling*. God provides everything needful and then calls us to respond. He spreads the table with good things and then invites us to come, to feast, to pray.

God wants you to pray. Let's dwell on that. The Almighty delights in your approaching him. He invites you, waits for you, welcomes you when you come. As you undertake to pray, he is your partner in the enterprise—the ultimate Senior Partner! When you purpose to pray more and better, he's there cheering you on. When you resolve to make prayer a central part of your life—a major commitment—he backs you up. It's his idea, his program. He is surely pleased when you begin to make it yours!

Because of all that, ordinary people can begin to look on praying as their life-mission. Elderly people, yes. Bedridden ones, surely—but not only those whose days of vigorous activity are past. Some busy men and women with considerable responsibility actually see prayer as their chief work. For them it has become a crucially important ministry.

If that hasn't yet become true for you, I deeply hope that it will. I hope that you will gain such a sense of prayer as God's gift that you will accept it as your calling. I hope that you will become so gripped with its importance, so excited about its possibilities, that you will invest yourself in regular, purposeful praying. At the end of each chapter there are "exercises" for your use in either private study or a group situation.

How can anyone express the difference that could make—without seeming to exaggerate? Some of the changes may be subtle, others quite dramatic. How can we describe what one life given to prayer could mean for the in-breaking of God's kingdom? How can we give any clear sense of what one person's intercessions may bring to a host of others? How can we begin to estimate what fulfillment there can be, what genuine joy, in a growing experience of communion with God?

We can't do that adequately, of course—at least I can't. But it seems to me well worth our best efforts. God knows that the world needs praying people! H. R. Rookmaker, a perceptive student of contemporary culture, observes that "the decay we see around us can be halted only when with God's help and a life of prayer we appropriate the power of Christ's resurrection to live as renewed human beings" *(The Creative Gift).*

PART 1

GOD'S GIFT

1

God's Name
Father

When you pray, say: "Father..." (Luke 11:2).

The right way to pray is to stretch out our hands and ask of One who we know has the heart of a Father.

Dietrich Bonhoeffer

We want to pray. We are ready to be learners in our Lord's school. What is the first lesson? Where do we begin?

There can be no doubt about that. We begin with *God*. Prayer doesn't start with our initiative. It's not a device to get his attention. Prayer is my answer, your answer, to God's call.

In the next four chapters, we'll explore that theme: God "beforehand" with us. He has spoken; he has acted; he has come. More than that, he is speaking still, working now on our behalf, drawing near to us. That's what makes our praying possible. That's what fills our feeble prayers with unimaginable life and power.

Do you realize all that God has done so that you and I can call on him freely in prayer? He is the gracious, active, self-giving One. He has revealed to us his *name;* he has provided for us a *way;* he has breathed into us his *Spirit;* he has left with us his *Word.* And he has lavished all of that on us in the supreme gift of his *Son,* Jesus Christ.

Think now with me about God's name. In the thought world of the Bible, a name is more than a series of sounds and syllables, more even than a title. A name says something about the person who bears it. It may reflect the circumstances of one's birth or a marked personality trait. At the deepest level, it describes character. When an individual like Abram, Jacob, or Simon the fisherman has a life-transforming encounter with God, he receives a new name. That is, he becomes a changed person.

God's name stands for his revealed character. It expresses the heart of what he has made known about himself. To learn God's name is to know his person. To call on his name is to invoke *him.* God's name is God himself, opening his heart to us. In his name, he stands revealed.

When Jesus' disciples asked him, "Lord, teach us to pray" (Luke 11:1), he responded with a name—God's name. That was what they needed to know first. Who is God? What is he like? How should I address him? Jesus said, "When you pray, say 'Father...'" (v. 2). That expressed, for Jesus, who God is.

Have you ever thought about how our "theology" affects our praying? Our deepest convictions about God usually determine the way in which we call on him. We venture to state it as an abiding principle: *As we believe, so we pray.*

That principle has been impressed on me over and over again in a seminary course that I have frequently taught. It's titled "The Theology and Practice of Prayer." In one assignment, each class member is required to report on the teaching of an influential philosopher or theologian. The student is to note, in particular, both that thinker's view of God *and* his understanding of prayer. The result is highly predictable. In every case, a close correlation emerges between the two. As we believe, so we pray.

Suppose your creed runs like this: "No God!" That obviously rules out prayer. What possibility can there be, on that view, of communion with a living Lord, of an "I-Thou" meeting—of pouring out your heart to Another? For atheists, prayer must seem utterly futile. We may cry out, but our voices die away in the void. We are like children coming back from school to an empty house. When we open the door and call plaintively, "Is anyone home?" no answer comes. We are greeted only with silence. No one is *there.*

No wonder prayer no longer has significance for many in our modern world! Paul Van Buren, a leader of the short-lived "God is dead" movement in theology, has tried to give it what he calls a "secular meaning." He writes in *The Secular Meaning of the Gospel,* "When ancient man prayed that God would send rain on his neighbor's field, he thought he was doing the most effective thing he could. Today," the writer continues, "he will...see what can be done to get water on the fields by irrigation or other means." Behold, prayer's "secular meaning"! It used to be a gesture of goodwill, but now we abandon it for more "practical" measures of our own.

When those same fields come to be nourished by the spring rain, who is there to thank? When I was traveling in the Soviet Union a few years ago, I picked up an attractive book called *Through the Eyes of Children.* These thoughts about agriculture and prayer struck me. "Several decades ago, hands were raised in supplication, praying for a good harvest. Today, transmission lines crisscross the land, bringing electric power to the countryside. The towers march off to the horizon...and the ears of grain of a new harvest bow low to the ground as if thanking *them* [italics mine] on behalf of the people."

You get the picture. Instead of praying, we discern what needs to be done and do it. Then, instead of thanking God, praising the Creator, we congratulate ourselves and pay homage to our own technology! That sounds crass, but what else can a thoroughgoing atheist say? That person's theology (or lack of it!) has already eliminated meaningful prayer. *As we believe, so we pray.*

Suppose you believe, as the ancient Greeks did, in a grim, inexorable Fate. Behind the passions and choices of gods and mortals, this relentless necessity keeps grinding on. It finally determines everything. Of what value then is prayer? You'll have to agree with the chorus in one of Sophocles's tragedies *Antigoné:* "Oh, pray not; prayers are idle; from the doom of fate, for mortals, refuge is there none."

If God to you is remote from human history, if he never intervenes, if he stands apart from life in this world, what requests can you hope to make of him? Surely none for daily bread, for help in distress, or for wisdom at a crossroads of decision. Your doctrine of God has made all such petitions seem fruitless. Your "God" is not in the business of doing that sort of thing. *As we believe, so we pray.*

Some of us hold more traditional views of God. We believe him to be the almighty Creator and Ruler of the universe, present in the world, active in our lives. But what do we most deeply believe about his attitude toward us? That may mold our praying more than any other single factor. Perhaps you are afraid of God. You fear that he dislikes and disapproves of you. You readily acknowledge that he's *able* to hear and help you, but you often doubt that he *wants to.* Prayer may be a promising option for others, perhaps, but not for you. To you, God's name has been "Heavenly Critic," "Almighty Truant Officer," "Divine Policeman." In your mind's eye, he is not smiling over you—but frowning, not holding out hands of welcome—but pointing the finger of accusation. What heart will you have to approach him, to open your whole being to him?

But now suppose that for you his name is "Father"? Suppose that you believe about him what Jesus believed. What effect will that have on your praying? Is it possible that you will begin to pray as Jesus prayed? Yes! *As we believe, so we pray.*

Jesus, the sources tell us, called God "Father" whenever he prayed. Notice his recorded prayers in the four Gospels. There are quite a number of them, and in every one he addresses God by that name. (The one exception is his cry of dereliction from the cross, "My God, my God, why hast thou forsaken me?" [Matt. 27:46]. And that, of course, is a direct quotation from Psalm 22:1.)

But here is a point of special interest. Jesus did not use the *ordinary word* for father, *abh.* He used instead the diminutive form *abba.* And, as far as we know, he was the first person ever to use that word *abba* as a name for God. In all of the Old Testament scriptures, in all the writings of the rabbis, in all the records of ancient Jewish prayer, there is not one instance of a worshiper addressing God as *abba,* points out Joachim Jeremias in *The Prayers of Jesus.*

Jesus' use of the term seemed so striking to them that the New Testament writers deliberately called attention to it. On several occasions, they brought this Aramaic word over into the common Greek of the day without translation. Other translators have continued that policy. On the shelves of my own library, for example, are Bibles in German, French and Spanish. In each one, at Mark 14:36, Romans 8:15, and Galatians 4:6, this untranslated *abba* is found. You'll notice the same thing, perhaps, in the English translation you are using. Do you catch the significance of that? This is the very word Jesus used! These are the syllables he uttered! In this little *abba,* we actually overhear the Savior of the world at prayer!

Abba was not an unfamiliar word in Israel. In fact, it was familiar—in the most literal sense. It came from the everyday language of a Jewish family. The first sounds an infant learned to make were *imma* (that meant "mother") and this baby name for "father"—*abba.* You know about names like that. Our family surely does!

My mother was born in south Georgia. She always called her mother "Mama" and her father "Papa." When I tried to say those names as a child, I couldn't quite get them right. My version for my grandmother was "Maa-Mah" and for my grandfather "Pap-poo." That's what I called them as long as they were alive. My grandmother died at ninety-nine—still Maa-Mah to me! We never forget those endearing family names, that child language of the home. Incidentally, it keeps traveling down through the generations, though with slight modifications. By our grandchildren, my wife and I have been forever dubbed Mee-Maw and Poppa.

Why hadn't anyone used *abba* before as a name for God? The word must have seemed *too* familiar. God was the exalted LORD, whose name was too sacred even to pronounce. He reigned in such inconceivable majesty that he must "stoop down" to behold the heavens and the earth! He was the holy Creator; all of us his sinful creatures. Awe, reverence, self-abasement were the only fitting attitudes for any who would approach him. Israel called him *abh,* "Father" of the people he had chosen, Lord of the nation, but never *abba.* Who would dare to call the Almighty something like "Daddy" or "Pap-poo"? But Jesus did. And for him that new way of addressing God expressed a new kind of relationship to him. Jesus knew that he was the beloved Son. He spoke to his Father, accordingly, with perfect freedom and unquestioning confidence. Reverent trust was in his prayers, grateful awe, a consuming desire to obey, but never a trace of formality or distance. He approached God with eagerness, affection and overflowing joy.

Picture the tiny child of a great king as he comes to the royal throne. Others quail before the monarch, tremble in his presence, fear even to lift their eyes toward him. But not this little boy! He races across the throne room to his father, clambers up in his lap, reaches up tiny hands to stroke his beard. How does he dare? Because for him, the king is "my dad"!

Now for something truly astonishing. God wants *us* to approach *him* in that way! That's what it means that Jesus told his disciples, "When you pray, say: 'Father.'" He was including us in the family circle, teaching us the Father's name. This was more than a word for us to repeat; it was a relationship for us to share.

That is the "good news." That's the joy that rings and sings its way through the pages of the New Testament. That's what the early Christians were so breathlessly excited about. Listen to John: "To all who received him [Jesus], who believed in his name, he gave power to become children of God" (John 1:12). Hear Paul almost rhapsodize on the subject: "...in Christ Jesus, you are all the sons of God through faith.... And because you are sons, God has sent the Spirit of his Son into our hearts, crying 'Abba! Father!'"(Gal. 3:26; 4:6).

Think of what a human father will do for his child. I'll never forget what my dad did for me one Easter morning long ago. I was a frail six-year-old, gravely ill. After a serious surgical procedure, I had contracted a blood infection and had been moved to a hospital for contagious illnesses. I can remember nurses coming in at all hours of the day and night to take fresh samples of my blood. Both my arms and each of my fingers hurt from those punctures. None of the treatments I was given seemed to help. My condition worsened. Finally it was decided to try a series of blood transfusions. My dad volunteered; his blood was the right type.

In those days, blood transfusions were sometimes direct—from the donor's arm into the patient's. I remember how frightened I was when they wheeled me out of my hospital room. I dreaded what was ahead, thinking it would be another operation. But when I saw my dad, I wasn't afraid any longer. Soon he was lying on a bed right beside mine, and his lifeblood was flowing into my veins. On Easter morning, after that new blood, I began to move slowly toward recovery.

I've often reflected on that experience. It was a sign to me of how much my dad cared for me. He lived that caring in many other less dramatic ways, too. I got this message: there was nothing my dad wouldn't do for his son. He was ready to give me his blood, his life.

Since then, I've become a father of four sons. I know something of how my dad felt. My wife and I have seen one of our boys afflicted with encephalitis, left with serious handicaps. Then when he died at 24, another son became deeply distressed and went through a long period of inner anguish. I couldn't give to either, of course, anything like a blood transfusion to restore health. But I know how many times I found myself wishing I could give my right arm to Billy for his withered one, or take on myself some of Dave's pain.

You know what that's like, if you're a parent. Is there anything you wouldn't give or do or suffer for that boy, that girl of yours, if they really needed it? It's not that any of us are such noble parents. Most of the time we are bunglers in that high calling. Our selfishness gets in the way. We're often impatient and insensitive. We pass along our hangups. We can be hard people for children to live with, can't we? And yet, if they're in trouble, if they're crying out for help, we want to be there. They're ours, and we'd do anything in the world for them.

Why is it so hard for us to carry over that awareness into our thoughts of God? We can believe in genuine parental love, but we sometimes doubt that our heavenly Father will prove to be similarly kind to his children. Jesus shows us how laughably, pretentiously wrong we are. We have the order of things reversed. "If you then," he asks, "If you then, who are evil, know how to give good gifts to your children, *how much more* [italics mine] shall your Father who is in heaven give good things to those who ask him!" (Matt. 7:11). The point is not that God is a bit like a human father or mother, but rather that the highest reaches, the most magnificent expressions of their parental love give us only a glimpse of his Father heart.

For some of us, to hear God spoken of as Father is not reassuring. We have all had imperfect parents, and some of us grew up in homes where fathers were largely absent. You may not even be completely sure who your father was. Or, your memories of him may be mixed with pain, anger, and shame. He abused you, perhaps. He laughed at you, put you down. It seemed that he never had time for you. "God is like a father?" you ask. "Who needs a God like that!"

I don't want to minimize that huge difficulty. The word *father* can be for some of us so loaded with negative associations that it seems to hinder faith instead of helping it. But most of us have seen or known someone who fulfilled a father's role—who really played the part. Perhaps your mother, or someone who wasn't a parent at all, embodied the heart of it for you. Maybe you found in a grandparent, an uncle, or even an older brother, a kind of father figure. Maybe it was a pastor, a schoolteacher, a next-door neighbor, a friend of the family who took a special interest in you. Someone believing in you, someone giving, someone caring, someone supportive, was there when you had a need. That's what a father is meant to be.

A good friend of mine has told me how he was orphaned soon after birth. He lived in a long succession of foster homes. His earliest memories are of fear and hunger, cruelty, and exploitation. He never knew anyone who seemed like a parent to him until he came to know his high school coach. This man valued Steve as a person, and encouraged him to develop his abilities. The coach was both an authority figure and a caring friend. In him Steve experienced for the first time something of what it is to have a father.

Whatever your family experience may have been, try to focus on that significant person in your life who has given you what Steve's coach gave him. Who is it that has most looked out for you, most treated you as a well-loved son or daughter? Think of that person; cherish the best you found in him or her; and then remember the question of Jesus about the Father in heaven: *how much more?*

For Jesus and his followers, the prayer "Father!" was supremely a prayer of *trust.* It surely included reverence. In Jewish families, grownup sons and daughters continued to address their fathers as *abba.* They used the term as an expression of respect. But the groundtone of *abba*—its dominant note—was unquestionably confidence. Jesus expressed it in this prayer by the grave of Lazarus: "...Father, I thank thee that thou hast heard me... thou hearest me always" (John 11:41, 42).

God is a Father whose knowledge of our situation is all-encompassing. "Your Father knows what things you need," (*see* Matt. 6:32) said Jesus. The God who sees the sparrow fall knows every one of our struggles and sorrows, even keeps count of the hairs on our heads. We can trust his perfect wisdom.

He is completely sufficient for our every need. Jesus prayed in the garden, "Abba, Father, all things are possible to thee..." (Mark 14:36). At any cry of his own for help, the Father can dispatch "more than twelve legions of angels" (Matt. 26:53). We can trust his infinite resources, his almighty power.

But we can be even more assured of his unfailing goodwill. Surely the One who feeds the nestlings, who decks out lilies in spring attire, will care for his own children! A tiny bird fluttering downward matters to him, and we are of more value than many sparrows. We need not fear, Jesus tells us, for the Father wills to give us good gifts, to make us heirs of his kingdom. Even our foolish wanderings, our selfish ingratitude, cannot destroy his fatherly kindness. From every "far country," he welcomes back returning prodigals, and even invites pouting, surly, elder sons to the celebration. What a Father!

Maybe you find all of that desperately hard to accept. So much of your own experience and your observation of the world seems to deny it. Is God a loving Father, when cancer is eating away the life of your dearest, when cherished dreams fade, and disappointments multiply? "You say he cares about us when money runs out, when there are no jobs, when mothers watch their children slowly starve? Tell us about it! Wars, earthquakes, monstrous cruelty, hatreds that never die—does all that sound like a Father's world? I'd like to believe it, but...."

I have no easy answers for those anguished, terrible questions. They have often haunted me. So much suffering that seems meaningless, so many ugly wrongs, so much to outrage anyone's sense of justice! Who can believe in a loving Creator behind it all—in a God whose name is Father?

I don't think I could, if all I had to go on was what I see around me. I don't think a reasoned argument or a church's authority could convince me of it. To me, it's believable only because of Jesus Christ.

Suppose the parable of the prodigal son had been taught by someone else. It would still be a touching story, masterfully told. But could I know with assurance that it tells me something about *God?* Would I have reason to believe that *I* will ever be welcomed in that way? It would be wonderful to know that, of course. But, really...?

Jesus himself has made the Father known. John says that he has "exegeted" him (*see* John 1:18), brought him forth for all to understand and appreciate. How do I know that God seeks after lost ones, loves the most unlovely, rejoices over sinners who come home? Because that's precisely what Jesus did. That's how he dealt with people. He came at his own initiative into a world of tears and trouble. He fed the starving, healed the afflicted, stood with the despised, stepped across every social barrier. He met rampant evil head-on, threw his own life into the struggle, took our worst sorrows upon him. He laid down his life freely on our behalf, and then triumphantly took it again. He lived out here, on our planet, in our history, a love that would otherwise have been utterly incredible. And he said before he died: "...He who has seen me has seen the Father" (John 14:9).

When it's hard for you to call God "Father," to believe that he yearns over you more than the best earthly parent ever doted on a child, look at Jesus. Watch him, study him, dwell on him, bring him again and again to mind. See him healing, helping, gladdening, welcoming. See him suffering, dying for people like you. If you want to see the unveiled glory of the Father, look there—in the face of Jesus!

Can you imagine the difference it would make in your praying if you believed—deeply believed, steadily believed—that God is this kind of Father? That would be the end of your reluctance to approach him, your formal posturing, your guilty fears. You could *run* then into his presence and tell him all your heart.

In seeking to make your prayer life better, richer, that is surely the place to start. We can be told *ad nauseam* that we should pray more, but never be helped by that in the least if our view of God remains dim or distorted. *As we believe, so we pray.* It's true that more prayer can make God more real to us, but only if we have begun to know him truly. Keep learning of him in the Scriptures, seeing his fatherly smile in Christ, and prayer for you will bloom and thrive. In every moment of need and in the morning of each new day, let the prodigal's resolve be yours: "I will arise and go to my father..." (Luke 15:18).

For Response and Resolve

Whenever I pray, let me think of God as the marvelously gracious Father revealed in Christ.

For Reading and Meditation

Luke 11:1–13
Luke 15:11–32
Romans 8:28–32
2 Corinthians 1:3, 4

For Reflection and Discussion

1. Discuss and evaluate the theme: "As we believe, so we pray."
2. How does the biblical idea of a "name" differ from our ordinary usage?
3. Who has modeled best for you the biblical image of "father"?
4. How is your understanding of prayer and your approach to it affected by Jesus' use of *abba?*

2

God's Way
The Mediator

There is one God, and one mediator between God and men, the man Christ Jesus, who gave himself as a ransom for all... (1 Tim. 2:5, 6).

Christ also died for sins once for all, the righteous for the unrighteous, that he might bring us to God... (1 Peter 3:18).

When we begin to speak of God's Son, we have God's heart.

John Calvin

The God who has revealed to us his *name* has opened for us also a *way*.

How does it come about we can call the Creator of the universe "Father"? The biblical witness reminds each of us repeatedly, "...God is in heaven, and you upon earth..." (Eccles. 5:2). He is the Holy One, of "too pure eyes" even to look on evil; we are covered with its blemishes. He is the Giver of all good gifts; we are the often ungrateful recipients who somehow manage to forget him in the midst of them. He is the sovereign Lord; we are his unruly subjects. Isn't it the height of presumption to imagine that we can be on friendly terms with this God? That we can address him with the family word *abba?* It surely would be—apart from the Great Introduction.

Have you ever been introduced to a famous person? Our late son, Billy, once had the privilege of meeting

Jim Kaat, then one of baseball's outstanding pitchers. Jim was playing at that time for the Chicago White Sox. Picture this now: it was Billy's birthday, and seeing a White Sox game was already the best present he could imagine. Jim Kaat had provided box seats for him and his family, and arranged to meet him by the Sox dugout an hour before game time. Billy was trembling with excitement as we helped him down the concrete steps at Comiskey Park for that appointment. Right on schedule, Jim appeared, smiling broadly. He presented Billy with a major league baseball, autographed with his personal birthday greetings. Joy! Best of all, he shook Billy's hand and spent a few moments talking with him, man-to-man. We had borrowed three cameras for the occasion and took several pictures of our beaming son meeting the famous Jim Kaat. What a birthday! Billy never forgot it.

How did all that come about? It began with a tennis match. My partner and I were talking between sets about our children. I happened to mention that our Billy was an avid White Sox fan. What a happy surprise it was to discover that my tennis friend's wife was Jim Kaat's sister! That gracious couple, Max and Esther, arranged the whole outing I've just described. They made possible what otherwise would never have happened. They, because of who they are, introduced our son to one of his sports heroes. How glad and thankful we all felt about that! It's a rich gift when someone you know can introduce you to a special person.

Surely the most significant encounter that any of us could ever have would be a meeting with God himself. Can such a remarkable happening be arranged? Is there anyone who can set it up, who can put us in contact, who can introduce us to the Almighty?

Perhaps you're put off or puzzled by that question. "Why is an introduction needed?" you wonder. "Surely religious people need no such formalities. Can't we approach God when and as we wish? If God is on the side of right, won't sincere involvement in any good cause bring us near him? Don't the techniques of meditation and all the paths of earnest searchers lead toward him?" The mood of many in our time might almost be captured in this parody of an old text: "Find the Lord where you decide to seek him!"

The consistent witness of the Bible, however, is strikingly different. According to the prophets and the apostles, none of us can make our own way to God. The gulf of separation is too vast, the barriers too formidable.

But what if God should take the initiative? The gospel announces that he has done just that. God chooses to be met; he seeks fellowship with his human creatures. All the writers of Scripture testify that we are made for him. To meet him, to dwell in his presence, to know and love him—this is life's ultimate meaning for us. And he wants it to be so! In fact, this message of God "with his people" is the Bible's grand story. Long ago, at history's dawn, it was creature and Creator in happy communion. And at the end, a great voice from the throne will say: "...Behold, the dwelling of God is with mankind. He will dwell with them, and they shall be his people..." (Rev. 21:3).

We today, however, are living neither in "the Garden of Eden" nor in "the New Jerusalem." The Bible speaks also of banishment from the garden, and of those who remain "outside" the holy city. It tells the poignant tale of our revolt, our estrangement, our wandering. We have forfeited the fellowship with God for which we were made, and have shut ourselves out from the joy of his presence. Like children bent on running away from home, we have lost our way.

Still the Bible's dominant theme is reconciliation. Ever since sin shattered the bond between God and ourselves, he has been seeking to restore it. He wants us to know him. Reunion is his aim; redeeming love his master strategy.

First, he chose a people for himself—little Israel. Though they were few and lightly esteemed, though they proved stubborn and wayward, he came to dwell in their midst. Yet the very sign of his presence (a tabernacle in the wilderness, a temple in Jerusalem) brought a reminder of separation. The inner sanctuary, the special place of God's dwelling, was shut off from the people by a thick veil. Nor could anyone enter there but the high priest, and he only once a year to offer sacrifice for the sins of the people.

Do you see the significance of that? The entire structure of Old Testament worship was designed to express a twofold message: God seeks fellowship, but sin bars us from his presence. He is gracious, yet grieved. He is at once near to us and far removed.

Now for the thrilling message of the New Testament: "Christ also died for sins once for all, the righteous for the unrighteous, that he might bring us to God..." (1 Peter 3:18). The situation, says the apostle Peter, has radically changed. God has done something decisive. He has sent his Son to be the Reconciler. Jesus has died to save us from our sins. Once for all, finally and forever, he has removed the separating barrier between us and God. Matthew tells us that in Christ's death, "the curtain of the temple was torn in two from top to bottom..." (27:51). The decisive deed had been done to open the way, to lead us back home. An old communion liturgy says it like this: "He cried with a loud voice: 'My God, my God, why hast thou forsaken me?' so that we might be accepted of God and never forsaken of him." All this the Savior suffered "that he might bring us to God." That is the "Great Introduction."

Have we felt the marvel of this, the breathtaking surprise of it? God is perfect love, but we are selfish and sometimes hostile. He is just, but we have filled the world with our injustice. He is altogether trustworthy, but we are experts in pretending. What have we in common with him? What right have we to stand before his throne? No right at all.

Yet, because of Christ, we may dwell with him. We may call him "Father" and live under his smile. We may approach him freely, without fear or furtiveness. We may know his cleansing and the quiet inflow of his strength. We can have a heart now to praise him, to love him, and to serve his purpose in the world. By the power of his Spirit, we begin to bear his likeness, and communicate his riches to those around us. All this because Christ has "brought us to God."

This was not an original idea with Peter. He learned it from his Lord. Jesus taught repeatedly that he, in his saving mission, was decisive for each person's relationship to God. To see him was to see the Father; to know him, to know the Father. To believe in him was to believe in the One who had sent him; to receive him meant receiving his Father. In fact, none could come to God except through him. None could even know the Father except those to whom he, the Son, would reveal him. "I am the way..." (John 14:6). He taught, "I am the door; if anyone enters by me, he will be saved..." (10:9). According to Jesus, the One who had sent him, the God he called Father, could be met and worshiped, served, and rejoiced in, only through him.

In faithfulness to Jesus, as witnesses to him, the apostles preached that message everywhere. Peter told the religious leaders of his nation, "There is salvation in no one else, for there is no other name under heaven given among men by which we must be saved" (Acts 4:12). Paul announced to his hearers: "through this man [Jesus] forgiveness of sins is proclaimed to you" (13:38).

"There is one God," he maintained, "and one mediator..." (1 Tim. 2:5)—one goal, one way, one Father, one
Savior. The people of God, the host of the redeemed, can
all be described in the letter to the Hebrews by this vivid
phrase: "those who draw near to God through him..."
(7:25).

Why do I say so much about this in a book on
prayer? Because here is the firm ground on which all
Christian praying rests. We come to God through Jesus.
We call God "Father" and draw near his throne because
of his self-offering. He is our Intercessor, our Intro-
ducer. He takes us by the hand, as it were, and brings us
before God.

Visitors to Catterink Camp in England are often impressed by a painting displayed there depicting a scene
from World War I. A *signaler* lies dead in no-man's-land
beyond the trenches. He had been sent out to repair a
cable cut by artillery fire. Though prostrate now in death,
he has fulfilled his task. In clenched hands he joins once
again the cable's broken ends. Written under the picture
is one word: THROUGH.

What a moving parable of Christ and his sacrifice for
us! Sin had blasted apart the lines of communication
between God and man. Jesus in death brought the
strands together and made contact possible again. Because of him, people like us can reach God. Those who
had lost contact with heaven now "get through."

What does it mean that Christians end their prayers
with phrases such as these: "In Jesus' name," "for
Jesus' sake," or "through Jesus Christ our Lord"? Such
words, of course, can be used mechanically, merely out
of habit. But they point to an ever-fresh reality. Believers
pray as those who are *united* with the risen Christ, vitally
joined to him by the power of his Spirit. They are members of his body. They pray also as those *identified* with
him and his cause in the world. Asking "in his name"

always involves commitment to his purpose. But for
us to pray "in the name" of Jesus, "for his sake," or
"through" him, means above all that we are *indebted* to
him for the privilege.

That is the keynote of New Testament religion: we
have free access to God, all because of Christ. Christians
who are bold to say, "Abba!, Father!" owe that marvelous privilege entirely to Jesus, the Son. In all their
approaches to the throne, they plead one name: they
depend on one sacrifice.

Remember the prayer of the despised tax collector in
Luke 18:13: "God, be merciful to me, a sinner"? Recent
studies suggest that what Jesus pictures here is more
than a plea for clemency. This prayer hints at sacrifice, at
atonement.

The tax collector, along with the Pharisee, his counter-
part, had gone up to the temple to pray. In all probability,
such a man would have attended temple worship at the
time of the afternoon sacrifice. There, at the climax of
public worship, an offering was made for sin. The transgressions of the people were confessed, and symbolically
transferred by the priest to a sacrificial animal. Then the
life of the beast was taken, as a divinely appointed substitute. In the afternoon sacrifice, worshipers beheld a kind
of sin bearing, a sign of God's saving mercy.

Put the tax collector's prayer in that setting and you
begin to see it in a new light. His petition was, quite
literally, "God, be made favorable toward me" or "Let
this sacrifice avail for me." He rested all his hopes on the
mercy of God revealed in that symbolic act. And, according to Jesus, he went down to his house justified, forgiven, accepted.

Jesus was teaching us in this parable, as in this entire
section of Luke's Gospel, how we are to pray. In the
Pharisee we see how *not* to approach God. What was

wrong with his prayer? Much about it seems commend-able. He expressed gratitude, "God, I thank thee..." (v. 11). The acts of service and piety he reported were impressive, to say the least. But in all his praying, we find no acknowledgement of sin, no awareness of grace, no dependence on the saving work of God. This man asked for nothing; he received nothing. While the tax collector went down to his house "justified" (v. 14), rightly related to God, this Pharisee remained as he was.

We pray rightly, we pray Christianly, when we come to God in the spirit of that nameless tax collector. We hope in God's mercy. We rely on his saving action. We look by faith to Jesus Christ, crucified for us, risen, and interced-ing on our behalf. "Let this sacrifice avail for me," we are asking. "I trust in Jesus as my sin bearer, my Savior. Hear me in mercy, for his sake." That's what it is to pray "through Jesus Christ our Lord."

Here's the key issue: on what basis do we come before God and call him "Father"? Is it in our own name, or in Jesus' name? Is it because of our worthiness to be heard, or his? Is it by a means that we have devised or by the way he has provided? In short, is prayer my right or his gift?

Think how much our *confidence* in praying hangs on this issue! If God's hearing and answering my prayer depends on my being good enough, working hard enough, proving worthy enough, what hope can I have? Assurance, on that basis, is out of the question. Even when I am most self-deceived, I can hardly build with firm confidence on that foundation. But what if every-thing, everything, depends on him? What if Jesus is the beloved Son, in whom the Father has been well pleased? What if his perfect sacrifice has blotted out all my sins? What if I come in his name, cleansed by him, clothed about with him? What if God, when he looks at me, sees only Christ, my Advocate? Or when he listens to my prayers, hears the voice of his own Son? Then I can be *sure.* Christians sing about it:

> The Father hears him pray, the dear Anointed One
> He cannot turn away the presence of his Son.

Will you join me in resolving to offer your every prayer "in Jesus' name"? Not that you will always use that phrase, or another like it. But let your purpose be to remember Jesus Christ and his self-giving love whenever you call on God. You can say "Our Father" because of Jesus, the Son. You have a share in the family inheritance because you are a "fellow heir" (Rom. 8:17) with him. He has introduced you; he has brought you home. Whenever you come to God, you come—oh, remember it!—through him.

For Response and Resolve

Whenever I pray, let me remember that the privilege of approaching God has been given me through Christ and his sacrifice.

For Reading and Meditation

John 10:1–9
John 14:1–6, 12–14
1 Timothy 2:1–7
Hebrews 4:14–16

For Reflection and Discussion

1. What stands in the way of our approaching God?
2. What has God done to open the way?
3. Evaluate other proposed "ways" into God's presence.
4. What does it mean to pray "in Jesus' name"?

3

God's Power
The Spirit

Likewise the Spirit helps us in our weakness; for we do not know how to pray as we ought, but the Spirit himself intercedes for us with sighs too deep for words. And he who searches the hearts of men knows what is the mind of the Spirit, because the Spirit intercedes for the saints according to the will of God (Rom. 8:26, 27).

This profound conception of prayer as the Divine in us appealing to the God above us is of a piece with Paul's whole doctrine of the Christian life. . . .

C. H. Dodd

Our first work, therefore, ought to be to come into God's presence not with our ignorant prayers, not with many words and thoughts, but in the confidence that the Divine work of the Holy Spirit is being carried on within us.

Andrew Murray

Prayer is God's gift. He reveals to us his *name* "Father." He opens for us a *way* through his Son. But there is more. He also breathes into us his *Spirit!*

The pastor's wife took me by surprise with her frank question. I was a seminary graduate student, teaching a class in the Christian faith and life at a nearby church. The time had come to deal with the doctrine of the Holy

Spirit. I had scarcely begun when my questioner arose,
puzzled and clearly impatient. "I can understand about
God the Father and Jesus," she blurted out, "but why do
we have to have this *Spirit?*"

I've wondered since if she spoke for a number of others
who might not have raised the issue so openly. Many
church people seem confused, uncertain about how to
understand the Spirit and his work. We've all had fathers; we can grasp something at least of what God's
fatherhood might mean. And Jesus, of course, lived
among us a life which, though unique, was thoroughly
human. We can know him as our brother. But how shall
we think of a Spirit whose being is mysterious, whose
operations are invisible—strangely elusive?

Our mentors in the faith haven't always helped. Some
say very little about the Spirit, seeming to relegate his
ministry to a bygone age. Others refer to him with great
familiarity, but chiefly in connection with mystical experiences and unusual phenomena. The question of that
pastor's wife may occur to us more than once. We're
average persons, living fairly normal lives. "Why do we
have to have this *Spirit?*" And especially, for our pur-
poses now, "What does the Holy Spirit have to do with
our prayers?"

The Gospel writers, especially Luke, make frequent
mention of the Spirit in connection with Jesus' ministry.
At the time of his baptism, the Spirit is said to "descend
upon" him (Luke 3:22). As he returns from that experience at the Jordan River, he is "full of the Holy Spirit"
(4:1). He is then "led by the Spirit" (v. 1) into his time of
wilderness temptation and returns from it "in the power
of the Spirit" (v. 14). When his disciples came back from a
missionary tour with good news, he "rejoiced in the Holy
Spirit" (10:21). We gain the impression that his entire life
is under the Spirit's direction and control.

This seems to be vitally related to his practice of
prayer. The coming of the Spirit on him at his baptism

occurs while Jesus is praying. As he carries out his ministry with the Spirit's anointing, each step of obedience,
each breakthrough of God's power, seems to be preceded
by prayer. It becomes clear that the fullness of the Spirit
is not a static condition for Jesus, but a dynamic process—a continuing renewal that is somehow related to his
prayerfulness.

He assures the disciples, at least, that it will be so for
them. The Father who is in heaven will give the Holy
Spirit, Jesus promises, "to those who *ask* him!" (11:13,
italics added). And that word *ask* is in the present tense,
implying a *continued* action. The followers of Jesus will
receive the Spirit's fullness and empowering, in other
words, as they "keep on asking."

They took that promise to heart. When Jesus told
them to wait in Jerusalem until the Holy Spirit would
empower them to be his witnesses, they understood
"waiting" to mean "praying." Luke tells us that the
whole company of Jesus' disciples "with one accord devoted themselves to prayer" (Acts 1:14). And on the Day
of Pentecost, sure enough, they were filled with the Spirit
and began their dynamic witness.

And that wasn't an isolated occurrence. Later on,
when the bitter winds of persecution began to howl
around them, these embattled believers gave themselves
again to prayer. And once more, "...they were all filled
with the Holy Spirit, and spoke the word of God with
boldness" (4:31). As the church's missionary advance
continued, this fact became luminously evident: when
Christians pray, the Spirit works. He is given, again and
again, in response to the petitions of God's people. Believers, like their Lord before them, are to be "filled with
the Spirit" (Eph. 5:18). They are to keep on praying *for*
the Holy Spirit.

But that isn't the whole story. The same Spirit who
came on Jesus at the Jordan to equip him for his ministry

had been at work in him throughout his life. Even as Jesus asked for the Spirit, he was being moved by the Spirit. The God who answered Jesus' prayer had himself inspired it. Prayer begins with the Spirit's quickening breath.

If there has been a birth in your family lately, you will know that hospitals these days are showing much more consideration to expectant fathers than they used to. At least that has been my observation. We've had four children, all grown now, but I've never yet seen the inside of a delivery room. I was always made to feel like a dangerous intruder when I wanted to be there—to get involved. But the last time my son became a father, they treated him as though he owned the hospital. They conferred with him in advance, explaining everything as carefully as if *he* were going to give birth. When the time came, they dressed him up in doctor's green and ushered him into the operating room. This was to be a Caesarean section, mind you, but that was no problem. Jim could be there, right at Kathy's side. He could even take pictures of the whole thing! How I envied him! I had gone to the hospital with him, to give him support, but now he was right where all the excitement was going on. *I* was the one pacing the halls outside!

But just hearing about things later, and seeing those altogether amazing photographs, made me forget about being excluded. The most unforgettable moment came, I am told, when little Anna Christine first emerged. Throwing up her arms as though to say, "Hello, world!" she let out a loud cry. At that, Jim cried. Kathy cried. Maybe the nurses and doctors cried, too—I don't know. There's something about that first sound that gets to everyone. It means *life.*

But before that tiny girl could sound off, she had to get her lungs full of air. First inhale, then exhale. You have to take in oxygen before you can let out a yell. And before you and I can breathe out a real prayer, God must breathe into us his Spirit. And that cry of ours, when it comes, is a sign that we are really *alive.*

We've been thinking about the wonder of God's father-hood, how through Christ we can be his sons and daughters, and call him by the family name *Abba.* Do you know how that child's prayer originates? Listen to Paul the apostle: "Because you are sons, God has sent the Spirit of his Son into our hearts, crying, 'Abba, Father!'" (Gal. 4:6). Before you cry, the Spirit cries. Before you pray like a child, God first sends to your heart the Spirit of sonship and daughterhood. It's when he imparts his life-giving breath that you can cry from the heart, "Father!"

The Spirit brings Christ to us. Always remember that. Many and varied are his gracious ministries, but this is central to them all. The Spirit joins us in a vital bond to Jesus, making us partakers of him. Through the Spirit, we are born anew, born from above, because the Spirit unites us to the Lord of life! The Christian life is Christ himself, living in us by his Spirit. And Christian prayer, at its heart, is Christ praying in us, "Abba! Father!"

Now that can easily be misunderstood. I'm not speak-ing of a kind of "possession," a displacement of our personality. It is we who live; it is we who pray, not some divine person substituting for us. We ourselves cry, freely, gladly, "Father!" But the new life which that prayer expresses is not of ourselves. It is God-given. We are beginning to breathe the air of heaven. Christ is beginning to be formed in us. We, with all our continuing humanness, are yet being transformed within, recreated in his image.

How can you tell that the Spirit is at work within you? Listen to Paul again: "...When we cry, 'Abba! Father!' it is the Spirit himself bearing witness with our Spirit that we are children of God" (Rom. 8:15, 16). Are you begin-ning to realize that God is your Father—that you are one of his beloved children? That is the Spirit's work. Do you trust in Jesus as the One who died for your sins that he might bring you to God? The Spirit gave you that faith. Do you find growing within you the confidence that God is *for* you, that nothing can ever separate you from his love? Rejoice, because it means that the Holy Spirit has poured that assurance into your heart. And every time you pray from the depths, "Abba! Father!" you can be sure that the Spirit was there before you, inspiring that prayer and sharing in it.

Paul has other things to say about the Spirit's work in our prayers. He not only inspires them within us; he also guides and helps us in formulating them. Listen: "Likewise the Spirit helps us in our weakness; for we do not know how to pray as we ought..." (Rom. 8:26). All of us know about that "weakness," don't we? Many times we feel unable to pray. We hardly know what to ask for. Sometimes we can't seem to get in touch with what it is that we most deeply need. We feel powerless to spread our situation before God. How good it is to know that the Spirit "helps" us, or literally "takes hold together" with us in our weakness! The image in this unusual Greek word is that of someone standing on the other side of a burden too heavy for us to lift alone. He gets under the load with us, helping us to carry it.

But his help goes deeper still. Sometimes our weakness is so profound and the pressures on us so distressing that we cannot pray at all. Our hearts cry out in pain, in longing, but our voices are silent. In the grip of cancer, or some desolating grief, when tragedy leaves us numb or failure drenches us with shame, we have no words. We can only groan.

The apostle Paul has been describing in this passage how the whole created order seems to groan. The entrance of evil into God's good world has brought all his beautiful handiwork under bondage to decay and futility.

All creation is sighing now, waiting on tiptoe for release, for fulfillment. The cosmos yearns for the day of all days when God's purpose will be accomplished, when the children of God will shine forth in his splendor.

Believers share that wordless groaning. They have received the firstfruits of the Spirit, the "downpayment" of their inheritance. They have tasted the life abundant of the age to come. They have seen glimpses of a glory yet to be. But they are still living a world full of evils, amid trouble and weeping. The tension builds for them between what is experienced and what is only longed for, between the "already" and the "not yet." They groan within themselves, and can lift toward God only "sighs too deep for words" (Rom. 8:26).

But precisely then, the Spirit "intercedes for us," with unutterable groanings. Think of that—the Almighty groans with us! God by his Spirit is in the midst of this sighing, suffering world, somehow sharing its pain and longing for its deliverance. He has come to dwell in the hearts of his people. When we are too weary, too stunned, too oppressed even to pray, he pleads from the depths on our behalf. He takes our scattered thoughts, our confused longings, and turns them into perfect prayer. And the Father who knows our secret hearts always hears that plea of the Spirit. In answer, he is at work amid all of life's circumstances for our good. He is making what seems so wrong to be somehow "all right" again.

Does the sheer miracle of that come home to you? It's staggering to imagine God coming to us; God feeling with us; God echoing our sighs, entering into our pain. But it happens. The incarnate Lord comes anew by his Spirit to share our lot and to intervene.

It makes me think of what friends did for us on the day our oldest son Billy died. I had heard him in the bathroom at 6:30 that morning, and had gotten up to help him back to bed. When I went to his room an hour later to wake him up for work, he couldn't be roused. We called the emergency medical team and they were at the door in a few minutes. Young Kris, strong and gentle, ministered to Billy for a quarter of an hour, trying to revive him. His evident caring moved us.

Others began to arrive. One look at the pain and sorrow in Al's face, and I knew that this neighbor of ours was really with us. Garry came, grieving, sensitive to what we were feeling. He said little, but gave us the gift of his supportive presence. Ron and Don, two faithful pastors, dropped in to let us talk and to offer prayer. Then there was Kurt. He noticed that we hadn't eaten that morning, and soon brought out from the kitchen a steaming, savory omelet! Evelyn and Dolores, bless them, put through the telephone calls that we were scarcely able to make. We felt wonderfully loved. Here were people seeking us out, weeping with us, doing simple things we had no heart to do. And so the Spirit, the very Spirit who dwells in those priceless friends, visits us in struggles and sorrows, sympathizing, listening, nourishing, even getting our messages through!

"Why do we have this *Spirit?* " We can say something about that now, can't we? Something about prayer. The Spirit: God's best answer to our unwearied asking, the only fullness that satisfies. The Spirit: God's own breath by which we live and pray, our helper and Guide. The Spirit: God suffering with us in the worst of times, praying from our hearts when we can barely groan. That's who he is. That's a glimpse at least of why we need him.

How shall we honor the Spirit in our praying, how respond to his work? See if this sounds to you like a fitting resolve: in my every prayer I will seek to *depend on the Spirit.* Let me remember how living prayer comes from him; let me wait on him for quickening and direction; and let me trust that he is there, on my side, pulling for me, when I'm too weary or weak even to cry, "Help!"

For Response and Resolve

Whenever I pray, let me depend on the Holy Spirit to guide me, help me, and intercede within my heart.

For Reading and Meditation

> Luke 1:11–13
> Romans 8:12–17, 26–27
> Ephesians 6:18–20
> Jude 17–21

For Reflection and Discussion

1. If we have received the Spirit, why must we continue to ask for his fullness?
2. In what sense is the prayer *"Abba!"* the Spirit's prayer? In what sense is it ours?
3. How does the Spirit "help" us in our prayers? How will you seek his help?

4

God's Word
The Promise

Let me hear what God the LORD will speak...
(Ps. 85:8).

The richness of God's Word ought to determine
our prayer, not the poverty of our heart.

Dietrich Bonhoeffer

One spring some years ago we had unexpected guests. A family of robins built their nest just outside our kitchen window. We could stand at the sink and watch them from only a few inches away. That, as you can imagine, generated great excitement among our sons. They showed unprecedented enthusiasm for washing the dishes!

Fascinated, we all looked on as the new robins appeared and grew. First, four eggs, startlingly blue against the drab gray of the nest. Then, one after another, the little birds broke their shells and squirmed free. Then began a remarkable process. The parent birds flew tirelessly forth and back to provide nourishment for their nestlings. It's almost beyond belief how many worms a tiny bird can consume. I'm told on good authority that some eat two hundred in the course of a day!

What I remember most vividly is the feeding operation itself. As soon as one of the "worm-bearers" hovered near, all four baby robins, as if on signal, opened their bills wide. I can hardly describe to you how *wide* that was. The angle of the spread had to be well above 90 degrees. The yawn seemed bigger than the bird!

Sometimes little children "open up" in a similar way, but not always. You may take a spoonful of cereal, fruit (or whatever mush babies eat these days), and bring it to your son's mouth with the cheery words "Open wide!" only to be disappointed. He doesn't open wide. He doesn't open, period. Maybe he gets an impish glint in his eye and shakes his head. That can be frustrating. Here you have this nourishing (if not tasty!) morsel all prepared. He needs it to grow, to be healthy and strong, but he won't eat it. The only thing more vexing is to see him take the food reluctantly and then reject it with gusto!

Those images flash through my mind when I ponder this biblical text:

> I am the LORD, your God, who brought you up out of the
>   land of Egypt.
> Open your mouth wide and I will fill it (Ps. 81:10).

God apparently has gifts for his children which they sometimes refuse to take. He offers nourishment for which they often show little appetite.

What is this food from God, this bread for the heart? The rest of the psalm makes that clear. God has something to *say* to his people. He wants to impart his *Word.* Hear this almost poignant outcry: "...O Israel, if you would but listen to me!" (v. 8). And again, as though God were musing within himself, "O that my people would listen to me...!" (v. 13).

If there is one theme that has vividly impressed me in my recent study of the Scriptures, it is this intense desire of God to be *heard.* He calls insistently through his prophets: "Land, land, land, hear the word of the LORD!"

(Jer. 22:29). His most frequent indictment against a wayward people is this:

> "...when I called, you did not answer,
>   when I spoke, you did not listen" (Isa. 65:12).

He searches everywhere to find someone who gives
heed, some openhearted listener,

> "...this is the man to whom I will look,
>   he that is humble and contrite in spirit
>   and trembles at my word" (Isa. 66:2).

We can appreciate a concern like that, can't we? If we
have something urgent to communicate—something
within us burning to be shared—how much it means to
find an authentic listener! We've all had enough of those
who seem to hear but remain preoccupied; who pretend
to be interested, but look for an opportunity to slip away;
who peer beyond us or smile vacantly when we crave to
be understood. Those of us who preach or teach confront
some in our congregations or classes who seem to gaze
off mindlessly into space, who whisper to one another,
who nod sleepily. But we mustn't look at them for very
long. That can be distracting—and discouraging! No, as
we scan those faces in the crowd, let's find one here and
there to whom our words seem important. Give us a few
listeners who lean forward, who give us keen attention,
who devour what we have to say. Then what a joy it is
to speak!

The more our message means to us, the more urgent
our passion for a hearing. I once had the chilling experience of being ignored when I tried to relate a deep family
sorrow. I was in a clinical pastoral training group at a
psychiatric hospital. Our program included a number of
experiments in communication. One day I was asked by

our group leader to share some thoughts at a staff gathering. Billy's handicaps were much on my mind at the time, and I decided to tell how his illness had affected our home. Without my knowledge, all the members of the audience had been previously instructed to show complete lack of interest! The design was to demonstrate how such nonverbal feedback could affect a speaker's ability to communicate. Oblivious to all that, I began to tell our story.

A man in front of me shifted uneasily. Another sighed and looked down. A third folded his arms wearily and looked out the window. As I told about our son's encephalitis, about his paralysis and his seizures, I began to feel almost sick. No one was looking at me! No one, that is, except Stan, a rugged, curly-haired seminarian. He was staring right at me, hanging on every word. That spared me, I think, from breaking down. For the rest of my talk, I looked straight at Stan. I told my story directly to him, and managed to finish. Stan, bless his heart, had recognized what was happening and decided not to go along with the experiment. What a gift he gave me!

God's chief concern in communicating is our good. He doesn't need, as I did, to share a burden, to find understanding and support. He seeks to give himself, to make our lives full in his fellowship. "O that my people would listen to me..." (Ps. 81:13) he declares.

> "I would feed you with the finest of the wheat,
>   and with honey from the rock I would satisfy you"
>   (v. 16).

The banquet is spread when the Word is spoken. "O taste and see!" comes the call, "taste and see that the LORD is good!..." (34:8).

But strangely, tragically, his chosen ones give no heed. "My people," God laments, "did not listen to my voice; Israel would have none of me" (Ps. 81:11). They had no desire, seemingly, for the Word he brought—no hunger to know him. We are shocked at that, and shamed. Something rebellious in us, something perverse, doesn't want to give God a hearing.

If you've made a serious effort to maintain a daily discipline of Bible reading, you know how surprisingly difficult that can be. There almost seem to be forces conspiring to keep us from it. A host of plausible reasons occur to us for neglecting it: We're so busy; we have things on our minds; life moves at a hectic pace and pelts us with interruptions; we scarcely have *time* to concentrate on God! And when we do open the Scriptures, how easy it is to read without a listening spirit, without an openness to God's message! We can comfortably sit through a sermon or a reading of Scripture without once wondering in our hearts, "Lord, what are you saying to me?"

The Old Testament prophet Isaiah described a coming Servant of the Lord who would react differently. He would listen. Here is one of his songs:

> ...Morning by morning he wakens,
>   He wakens my ear
>   To hear as those who are taught.
> The LORD God has opened my ear,
>   and I was not rebellious,
>   I turned not backward.
> I gave my back to the smiters,
>   and my cheeks to those who pulled out the beard;
> I hid not my face
>   from shame and spitting (Isa. 50:4–6).

We recognize that figure, don't we? Only One among us fully fits the picture. How he wakened to his Father's voice and heeded the call—even when it led him down a Via Dolorosa! Here is Jesus Christ: the obedient Servant, the loyal Listener. He said, "...I do as the Father has commanded me..." (John 14:31). The truth he leveled at the tempter was his meat and drink: "Man shall not live by bread alone, but by every word that proceeds from the mouth of God" (Matt. 4:4).

And he, the listening One, can make hearers of us. Do you remember his word in Mark 7:34 at the Sea of Galilee to a man who was deaf and dumb: *Ephphatha,* "be opened"? That's another of those untranslated utterances like *abba.* Jesus must have said it frequently, and it apparently took on special significance for his followers. The Lord said to a man whose hearing was blocked, whose ears were shut, *Ephphatha*—"be opened!" The disciples saw in that more than a deed of compassion, more than a miracle, more even than a sign of his lordship. It pointed powerfully to the meaning of his mission, to the deliverance he came to bring. Jesus the Healer gives light to the inwardly blind, cleansing for moral lepers, life to the spiritually dead. And he makes the deaf ones, heedless of God's call, to hear as never before. That's what *Ephphatha* means—he has opened our ears. And he does it not once for all, as a kind of permanent restoration, but "morning by morning." He wakens our ears "to hear as those who are taught" (Isa. 50:4).

That doesn't free us, of course, from the need and summons to *use* this new capacity. How often Jesus said it: "He who has ears to hear, let him hear!" (Matt. 13:9). As one set free to listen, you can train yourself in the high art. Have you noticed how you can *learn* to listen to the morning song of a favorite bird or the varied signals of a baby's cry? You can discipline yourself to listen to one voice among many in a crowded place. You can even shift your attention back and forth between two. You can so attend to a hurting person that you hear the rush of feeling behind the words. Yes, and you can learn to listen to God in such a way that you begin to take in what he wants to say to you.

There's another theme in that servant song.

> The LORD God has given me the tongue of those who are
>   taught,
> that I may know how to sustain with a word
> him that is weary (Isa. 50:4).

The Lord who gives ears to hear gives also a tongue to speak. It is no mystery that deafness and dumbness are often found together. We can frame into words only what we have heard. And the same mighty *Ephphatha* which creates our hearing also calls forth our speech.

That is profoundly true with regard to prayer. Think of what we have been considering about God's provision for it. How could we ever know that his *name* is Father; how could we find the *way* in Christ, how experience the Spirit's *help,* without the Word? The Word of God, incarnate in Jesus, proclaimed by prophets and apostles, written and preserved in Scripture, creates our hearing and calls forth our prayers. We pray in faith, we call on God in truth, only when we have first heard his voice.

What shall we say to the Almighty? In what spirit shall we come to him? How much we learn about that from one Bible book in particular: the Psalms! Martin Luther found these outpourings of the heart to be the Holy Spirit's chief resource in teaching us to pray:

> When the blessed Spirit of God, the Father of orphans and
> the teacher of the ignorant, sees that we do not know
> ...how to pray...He helps us in our weaknesses. As a
> teacher will compose letters or little speeches for his pu-
> pils to write to their parents, so by this book [the Psalter],
> He prepares both the language and the mood in which we
> should address the Heavenly Father (*Luther's Works,* vol.
> 14, p. 286).

What a vivid image—the Holy Spirit coaching us in our messages back home! In those psalms the Word of the

Father and the answering cry of his child come myste-
riously together. Echoing them, together with the Lord
who used them before us, we discover what it is to pray.

Every portion of Scripture calls for some response in
prayer. I read the commandments, and am moved to
confess my transgressions, to seek God's forgiveness, to
ask for strength. Reminded of God's greatness, I give
praise; of his mercies, I offer thanks. The more I grasp of
his purpose in this world, the more ardently and intel-
ligently I can pray for its fulfillment. But what especially
awakens faith and enables me to pray with confidence, is
his word of *promise.* It is God's promise on which faith
can build. It is his pledge that gives us courage to pray.

When King David had respite at last from war, he
decided to build a house for the Lord. He shared this plan
with the prophet Nathan. The next day Nathan returned
to the king with a divine message: God had a better plan.
He would build a house for David! Not a dwelling, of
course, nor a temple, but a dynasty. David was assured
that his line would long continue, that one of his descen-
dants would always reign over the house of Israel. That
was God's promise.

The king was overwhelmed. "Who am I, O LORD God,
and what is my house, that thou hast brought me thus
far?" (2 Sam. 7:18). It seemed to David almost beyond
belief that the Lord of heaven and earth should make him
such a promise. David gave himself up to wonder and
praise. Then this: "And now, O LORD God, confirm for
ever the word which thou hast spoken concerning thy
servant and concerning his house, and do as thou hast
spoken" (v. 25). Did you hear that: *Let your word be
confirmed. . .do as you have spoken.* David is basing his
prayer firmly on the promise, calling on God to make it
good. In fact, the promise has created the prayer, giving
David the heart to ask. "For thou, O LORD of hosts, the
God of Israel, hast made this revelation to thy servant,

saying, 'I will build you a house'; therefore thy servant has found courage to pray this prayer to thee" (v. 27).

Here we touch one of the basic issues in biblical prayer: *asking with faith.* Jesus said a great deal about that, didn't he? "Whatever you ask in prayer, believe that you receive it, and you will" (Mark 11:24). "If you have faith and do not doubt...according to your faith be it unto you" (*see* v. 23).

I've often pondered what that means. What is this faith that opens all doors, that unfailingly receives what it asks? Is it a psychospiritual feat, a supreme effort of soul by which we summon confidence that God will give us whatever we want? Will he do anything conceivable for me if I can banish all doubts and expect his gift with perfect confidence?

I long held that view, or something like it. If I could believe "hard enough" that my request would be granted—even shutting my eyes to contrary evidence—God would eventually respond. My prayer, when powered by such faith, would have a kind of delegated omnipotence.

The first chinks in that solid conviction began to appear for me in my experience as a baseball player. I was a pitcher (at least that was the position I played in high school and in college). In baseball jargon, however, I was more a "thrower" than a "pitcher." Pitchers have a good sense of where the ball is going when they let it go; throwers do not. Pitchers have "control"; throwers are characteristically "wild." When I wound up on the pitching mound and fired away, I was never completely sure what would happen. Sometimes the ball went skidding into the dirt; sometimes it sailed over the catcher's head. I was even known at times to throw pitches behind a hitter's back!

It was in the midst of my pitching career that I became a Christian. Assured by my spiritual guides that I should pray about everything, I began with petitions for accuracy as a pitcher. I can remember many occasions on which I breathed this prayer in the midst of a game, "Lord, help me to get this one over the plate!" Honesty compels me to say that it didn't always work out that way. Often the next pitch went elsewhere. I even established a kind of record at Davidson College for the highest ratio of bases on balls to innings pitched. I once walked 13 batters in 5-1/3 innings before being mercifully relieved!

The point is that I *believed* when I prayed those prayers. I had no doubt (at least in the earlier experiences) that my request would be granted. I *expected* to see the ball go straight toward the catcher's mitt when I released it. One could possibly argue that my wildness would have been even worse had I not prayed! But, at any rate, my conviction that I would forthwith become accurate, that I would have great "control," was not confirmed.

I've since made the same discovery in praying about much more important issues—healing for my mother when she suffered from cancer, and deliverance for one of my sons when he was partially paralyzed. I believed implicitly about these things, as did others. I once recorded in an interleaved Greek New Testament of mine the conviction that Billy's right arm would be completely restored. But it didn't happen. Nor did my mother recover.

Some would offer the "out" that my faith had not been strong enough or pure enough. I surely couldn't prove the contrary. But neither could I accept that as an explanation. It seemed too pat—and too heartless.

King David's experience has been a key factor in helping me to see "the prayer of faith" in a different light. I no longer believe that God will grant whatever I ask, merely because I happen to believe it strongly enough. "Faith,"

on that view, would be very much like manipulation—
pressuring the Almighty to do whatever I want. It would
almost be faith in myself—in my own power to pray
effectively, to believe successfully, to "do it right."
And that is quite different, it seems to me, from faith
in *God.*

In the Bible, faith is God's gift, quickened in our hearts
through his Word. I can truly believe that he will act in a
certain way, not because I think it probable or hope it
may be so, but only because he has made his will known.
*Faith is not believing that God will do anything imagin-
able, but rather that he will do whatever he has promised.* To believe in God is to regard him as reliable—true
to his covenant. We pray in faith when we echo David's
remarkable petition: "Confirm forever the word which
you have spoken...do as you have said." Jesus' words
"Have faith in God" (Mark 11:22) can more literally be
rendered, "Hold the faithfulness of God." That's it: cling
to the confidence that God is faithful. The Tzeltal Indians
in Mexico translate the biblical words *to believe* in a
vivid, moving way. Believing, in that culture, means
"holding on to God with your heart." And for that we
need a sure word from him.

God wants us, friends, to listen to him. By his loving
call, he opens our ears, and then urges us to use them. He
offers us the wheat and honey of his Word, inviting us to
"open wide." So that we may speak to him, he speaks
first, showing us how to approach him, even what to
say. He quickens faith and eagerness by his unfailing
promise.

Let everything for us, then, begin with listening. Let's
listen to the people around us, to their hurts and longings. Let's listen sensitively to the events of our time.
Let's hear the voice of God in the varied experiences he
brings us. Let's listen supremely to the Word he sends us
in Scripture, meditating on it day and night. That is the

richest kind of meditation. And whenever we prepare for prayer, let's commit ourselves to ask, like young Samuel: "...Speak, Lord, for thy servant hears" (1 Sam. 3:9).

For Response and Resolve

Whenever I pray, let me begin by listening to what God is saying to me through his Word, by his Spirit.

For Reading and Meditation

1 Samuel 3:1–19
Psalm 81:5–16
Psalm 119:9–18
Isaiah 50:4–6
Mark 7:31–37

For Reflection and Discussion

1. How does God's desire to be "heard" differ from ours?
2. What is involved in "learning to listen"?
3. How is faith related to God's promise?
4. In what ways can we "turn the Scriptures into prayer"?

PART **2**

OUR CALLING

5

The Call to Praise

Celebrating God

I will bless the LORD at all times; his praise shall continually be in my mouth (Ps. 34:1).

One of the most essential preparations for eternity is delight in praising God.

Thomas Chalmers

Now, friends, we are ready to pray! We know God's name: Father. We've found a way to approach him freely through his Son. His Spirit has come to be our Helper and Guide. We have listened to the Word he sends us. Now we draw near. What shall we say?

The prophet asked long ago, "With what shall I come before the LORD...?" (Mic. 6:6). In other words, how shall I begin my response, my answering word? Prophets and apostles, psalmists and saints of every age, answer in one accord: "Come with *praise.* Give God *glory.*"

Did you know that you could do that—that you could give God glory? *Glory,* in the language of the Bible, means both "brightness" and "heaviness." God's glory is the outshining of who he is, his revealed splendor. It is God's overwhelming majesty, his "weightiness," his infinite significance. Isn't it laughable to imagine that creatures of his could ever "give him" glory? It surely is, if by that phrase we mean "making him more glorious." Who could add to the luster of a God who keeps the heavens ablaze with stars? Who could make the incomparable Lord, on whom all things depend, more important than he is? But this we *can* do: as he reveals himself to us, we can become aware of who he is, of his glory, and *celebrate* him.

Did you ever make a sunset more beautiful? Did you ever brighten the splendors of a western sky? Of course not. But think how many sunsets you have celebrated. You gazed and gazed with unembarrassed wonder. You caught your breath. You couldn't help speaking, exclaiming, over what you saw. You had to call someone near you, even a stranger, and say, "Look! Look there!" Then you turned again to look for yourself, broke into a smile, shook your head admiringly, "What a sight!" You didn't enhance that sunset in the slightest, but how you celebrated it!

Now suppose that in those moments your heart leaped up in praise. "Lord, that's marvelous!" you cried, "How great you are!" In that you gave God glory. In the beauty of his handiwork, you celebrated, you enjoyed him. In that sunset you caught a glimpse of his glory and reflected it in joyful worship.

Worship means, literally, *worth-ship*. When we worship, we acknowledge worth. We don't create it or increase it; we simply recognize that it's there and respond accordingly. Worship is something like applause or cheering. When we clap or shout acclaim, we're saying, "This person deserves recognition," or "That performance was priceless." Our response is almost involuntary at those times; it comes pouring out of us. We *have* to get up on our feet, *have* to give expression to what we feel. And when we do, we enjoy it immensely. Smiling, beaming, we feel "good all over."

That is a key point, it seems to me. To praise is to celebrate; to worship is to enjoy. When we fail to see that, "giving glory to God" can be sadly misunderstood. God can be pictured then as a colossal egotist, forever commanding us to tell him how great he is. We resent others who demand that, don't we? And what contempt we sometimes have for the fawning crowd that seems to feed such vanity!

But what if a God of unimaginable love wants to make our lives complete, wants to give us joy, wants to communicate himself to us? And what if he knows that this can happen only in our worshipful response to him? Then his call to worship takes on a different sound altogether. To praise him is to partake of his fullness. To glorify God is, yes, to "enjoy him forever."

Not to praise God is to miss our destiny. The root of sin, according to the apostle Paul, is that we suppress what we know of the Creator and do not "honor him as God..." (Rom. 1:21). We act as though our Maker did not exist. All our thoughts are "No God." We give the honor due him to ourselves, or to images of our own making. We offer praise—all of us; indeed, we are inveterate "praisers." But we often lavish worship on "the creature rather than the Creator, who is blessed forever" (v. 25).

We want to worship, don't we? We delight to celebrate worth. See how a man extols some famous athlete, how a woman gushes over her favorite movie star. We glory in our race, our homeland, our beautiful women—anything we can contrive to call *ours*. We speak in glowing terms of whatever we think biggest or strongest, richest, or fastest. It rarely occurs to us that what we admire, what we congratulate, owes its being and beauty wholly to Another. We manage to forget the Giver even as we magnify the gift.

Now it's clear that *words* of praise to God are not the only forms of worship—not even the chief ones. Without devotion of heart and obedience of life, our words of praise are garish and empty. Trust, commitment, seeking for justice, compassion toward others—God looks for these in his worshipers. We glorify God on the earth, according to Jesus, by "accomplishing the work" (*see* John 17:4) he gives us to do. We are to *be* a people for his praise and to offer in worship our whole selves.

But the prophets and apostles, even as they denounce empty talk, never underestimate the importance of what we *say*. Hosea counsels a faithless people to turn from their vain, hypocritical ways of worship. But as they repent and turn, he urges, "Take with you words..." (Hos. 14:2). Words without heart are a hollow mockery, but when the heart begins to come around, words can speed it on its way. Let a woman resolve to praise God in her whole life, and she will find that frequent words and songs of praise can help to keep that purpose alive.

During my college years, I had great difficulty maintaining what is called a "devotional life." I had been told at the time I became a Christian that my joy and fruitfulness as a believer would depend in great measure on daily times of worship and communion with God. I learned—sometimes by disheartening experience—how true that was. But even after many lapses and defeats, I still seemed to lack the motivation and self-discipline to stay at my "devotions."

I talked to an upper-classman about it, a leader on our campus. He sympathized with me in my struggle, but urged me not to worry about it. If I didn't feel like reading the Bible or praying, if I wasn't inclined toward worship—I was not to blame myself but simply to wait until the desire returned. The advice was well meant, I'm sure, but proved less than helpful to me. To tell the truth, the less I prayed, the less I seemed to feel like praying. Something was wrong. The most important activity in life was being left at the mercy of my moods.

That, I suppose, is the fundamental issue. Is it *important* to praise God? Can this justly claim priority in

the ordering of our lives? Does it mean something significant to *him?* Does he value our praises? It certainly
seems so. Jesus says that God "seeks" those who will
worship him in spirit and truth. He commands his people
repeatedly to worship him, and him only.

The psalmists are so impressed with God's worthiness
to be honored that they set themselves to praise him all
their days.

> My heart is steadfast, O God,
>   my heart is steadfast!
> I will sing and make melody!... (Ps. 57:7).

> I will praise the LORD as long as I live;
>   I will sing praises to my God while I have my being
>   (146:2).

> Every day I will bless thee,
>   and praise thy name for ever and ever (145:2).

In the light of what they know of him, because of his
mighty works and steadfast love, they are determined to
keep on praising him, whatever their feelings. That
sounds fitting, doesn't it?

Alexander Whyte, a giant among Scottish preachers,
used to counsel his hearers to "think magnificently of
God" *(Lord, Teach Us to Pray)*. He felt that all genuine
praise arises from calling to mind God's greatness and
goodness. Reading Scripture, meditating on it, has this
as its grandest fruit. Beholding God's glory, with eyes of
faith, we are led to praise, to celebrate him. When God is
not in our thoughts, on the other hand, the wellsprings of
praise dry up. When we forget him "days without number," those days are devoid of real worship. But when we
think of him, think magnificently of him, when the riches
of his self-revealing fill our minds, praise flows freely
again.

To embark on a life of praise then is to desire that God
shall be in our thoughts, before our mind's eye. I want

each day to celebrate the fact that God is truly our Father in Christ. I want to *think* of how the Scriptures present him as Father, and then turn those thoughts to words of praise. They often come out something like this:

> I praise you,
> almighty Creator, God of covenant, holy Lord,
> > that you are also our Father.
> I praise you
> > that you encourage us in our trials.
> I praise you
> > that you are at work in all our circumstances for the best,
> > that you give us good gifts, that you chasten us in love,
> > that you welcome us back from all our wanderings with pardon and joy.
> I praise you, Father,
> > that you are *for* us,
> and that nothing can ever separate us from your love.

I find that simply thinking those thoughts afresh each day, forming those words, helps to make God's Fatherhood a living, bright reality to me. It helps me to celebrate who he is, to rejoice in his goodness. My response at the feeling level may vary with a number of factors, but I'm always heartened in remembering that God is *Abba,* and that I am one of his children. And because I'm a father myself (and a grandfather too!), and know how much the upturned faces of my children mean to me, how much I delight to hear them call my name, how it thrills me when they smile and say, "I love you, Dad!," "I love you, Poppa!," I can't help believing that our small praises somehow gladden God's heart, too.

I try to offer worship to the Son, our Lord Jesus Christ, in the same way. I bring to mind the living One to whom prophets and apostles bear witness, and turn their testimony into my own words of celebration.

I magnify you, Lord Jesus—
You are the Son of the Blessed, the everlasting Word;
You have made the Father known to us, you have given
  yourself for us, that we may have true life—
Now you are risen, exalted as Lord over all.
I worship you, Lord Jesus;
You are the friend of the friendless, the Savior of sinners.
You rule over and defend us—
You love us and intercede for us—
You're preparing a place for us.
Even now, you're with us all the days, never failing or
  forsaking us;
One day you will come in glory and power to receive us
  and to reign forever!
Lord, I rejoice in you.

Again, this is a way of seeking to "set the Lord always
before me," to keep him in view, to remember him. When
I call to mind that he is *worthy* to be praised, I find fresh
reason and motivation to celebrate him.
  And so with God the Spirit:

Holy Spirit, Lord and Lifegiver, sent from the Father and
  the Son,
I worship you—
You assure us of the Father's love—
You join us to Christ and to each other in one body—
You guide us into all the truth; you open the Word to us—
You help us to pray and praise—
You bestow upon us gifts for ministry and power for wit-
  ness.
I praise you, Holy Spirit—
You dwell within us, making our bodies your temple—
You bring the powers of the coming age into our experi-
  ence—
You are at work to conform us at last to Christ—
All praise to you, Spirit of the living God!

Even as I put down these thoughts, the reality of praise
I'm trying to describe seems eminently *right* to me all

over again. It *is* "a good thing" to magnify the Lord! He *is* "greatly to be praised!" Praise is comely, fitting, altogether appropriate. To celebrate him is supremely to give honor to whom honor is due.

I make no plea for my particular notes in the symphony of praise, still less for the words in which I try to express them. Let each, in bringing the Lord to remembrance, find his or her way to enjoy these riches, to let recollection rise as worship. But let's seek each day to "think magnificently" of God, and to celebrate him in praise!

Much is said in current devotional literature about the *power* of praise. We are reminded of how the servants of God under King Jehoshaphat went into battle singing to the Lord. "And when they began to sing and praise, the LORD set an ambush..." (2 Chron. 20:22) against their foes and gave them victory. When Paul and Silas prayed and praised God at midnight in a Philippian dungeon, the Lord sent an earthquake which led to their release (*see* Acts 16:25, 26). As these marvelous events are described and set forth as an example for us, I sometimes get the feeling that praise is being recommended as a *means to something else.* We are to worship God in our extremities of need *so that* his power will be released for our deliverance. The message comes through like this: "Praise God, and all kinds of remarkable things will happen in your situation."

Now I can rejoice as much as anyone at how God intervened for a beleaguered army or for Paul and Silas. But praise to God in each of those instances was an expression of living faith. The believers worshiped the Lord because he was *with them,* no matter what they had to face. They praised him because he is "great and greatly to be praised." Those who so praise God are often surprised and thrilled at what he later does. But those who praise him "for results," with an eye to what their praises will produce, may be disappointed.

When that is said, the fact remains that praise to God has significant effects upon us. It's like throwing open the windows of a stuffy room to let the fresh air of heaven in. It relieves the pressure of anxiety and helps us to see our problems in true perspective. It gets us out of preoccupation with ourselves and shifts our attention to the Lord. Best of all, it makes him more real to our awareness. It opens the way for him to give himself anew to us. In that sense, there surely is "power in praise."

Whatever we worship transforms us. We become like what we most admire. Paul can say this of communion with the risen Christ: "We all, with unveiled face, beholding the glory of the Lord, are being transformed into his likeness from one degree of glory to another..." (2 Cor. 3:18). Worshipers are scarcely conscious of that, just as Moses didn't know that his face was aglow from talking with God. *But they become different.*

Again, the people of God do not worship in order to become more Christ-like, anymore than they praise him to receive power. But every act of genuine worship makes us better persons, and finds us reflecting something of the Lord's image. The psalmist says it beautifully: "Look to him and be radiant..." (Ps. 34:5).

We are created for his glory. We are redeemed to show forth his glorious grace. We have life and breath to sing his praises. Let's join the chorus of creation, the hosts of heaven, and all the redeemed here in magnifying God's name. Let's hallow the whole of each day by devoting a part of it completely to adoration. Here's a great aim to share, a great calling to fulfill: "I will bless the LORD at all times; his praise shall continually be in my mouth" (34:1).

For Response and Resolve

Because God has created and redeemed me for his glory, let me set my heart each day to praise his name.

For Reading and Meditation

Psalm 145:1–3
Psalm 146:1–2
Psalm 150
John 4:21–24
Hebrews 13:7–15

For Reflection and Discussion

1. How can we "glorify" God?
2. In what sense is every human being a "worshiper"?
3. How can we come to "think magnificently" of God?
4. List, in order of their importance to you, significant reasons for praising God.

6

The Call to Thanksgiving
Remembering God's Mercies

Bless the LORD, *O my soul; and all that is within me, bless his holy name! Bless the* LORD, *O my soul, and forget not all his benefits (Ps. 103:1, 2).*

He who brings thanksgiving as his sacrifice honors me; to him who orders his way aright I will show the salvation of God! (Ps. 50:23).

Let never day nor night unhallowed pass, but still remember what the Lord hath done.

William Shakespeare

We were puzzled and hurt. We felt used, disappointed, somehow empty. My wife and I struggled to understand why we were so upset by the ingratitude of our houseguests. They had arrived earlier than we had expected and had stayed for a full week. Helen had prepared a succession of splendid meals for them, but they had never once commented on her cooking, even though I had tried once or twice to "prime" their appreciation with compliments of my own. We had taken them here and there, introduced them to friends, and spent some of our best evening hours trying to entertain them, all during a busy fall season. None of this, as I recall, was ever acknowledged in any way. One day, they simply left. Since then, and that was years ago, never a note, never a

71

call, never a sign that their stay with us had ever been thought of again.

Why did that rankle with us so? Did we dislike them, and begrudge the hospitality we had shown? No, we agreed that it had been good getting to know them and that most of our interactions during that week had been enjoyable. Did we feel the need to be repaid, or get something back from the investment of our efforts, our time? Perhaps, yet it's hard to think of anything we would have wanted them to give us—anything, that is, except a hint of gratitude.

It wouldn't have taken much. A smile of real delight, a word of appreciation, a little note to say they had enjoyed being with us—any of those would have made us feel immensely better. *Why?* we asked ourselves. Why was a bit of thankfulness so important to us, and the absence of it so disappointing?

It made me think of another experience we had had years before, with another houseguest. This man's name was Augustus. He was a Christian from Liberia who had come to speak at the church I was serving in Chicago. He was the first African believer I had met, and I was impressed both by his zeal for the work of Christ and his winsome, gracious manner. I still remember praying with Augustus (this was over twenty-five years ago) and rejoicing that two men as different as we in background, culture, and experience could feel such remarkable kinship in prayer.

I remember most vividly the letter he wrote after returning to his homeland. It contained an expression of thanks for our hospitality, but went far beyond that. The entire letter seemed to celebrate the miracle of gratitude. Augustus couldn't say enough, it seemed, about how marvelous it is to experience thankfulness. Then came this sentence which I shall never forget: "Even the death of our Lord Jesus Christ would mean no more to me than the death of a common housefly if I could not *appreciate* it." For him, the gift of God which made all others complete was a grateful heart.

I can't fully describe the effect on me of that visit and that letter. I know this at least: I was full of joy for having known Augustus and having felt the warmth of his thankful spirit. I recall that whole experience now, as I write about it, with a returning glow of peace and well-being.

Surely you've had similar experiences. You have felt, on the one hand, how painful it is to be disregarded or unappreciated. You can echo, perhaps, the wail of Shakespeare's *King Lear*: "How sharper than a serpent's tooth it is to have a thankless child!" Or you can agree with these words from *As You Like It*: "Blow, blow, thou winter wind! Thou art not so unkind as man's ingratitude."

But you've also been enriched, I trust, by someone's thankfulness. You've had a guest like Augustus to grace your table, receive your kindness, and then overwhelm you with the most charming, unaffected gratitude. That warmed your heart; that made your day.

Why? Why are all of us so deeply affected by the way in which others respond to our gifts and services? Why do expressions of thanks mean so much to us? Why does ungratefulness sometimes chill us and sadden us so?

I don't pretend to know the full answer to that, but I'm sure it has something to do with our desire to give ourselves—with our quest for relatedness. In our best moments, we give because we care, because we want to enrich another's life, to impart joy. We long to share what we have, to communicate something of ourselves. Gratitude, when it comes, means that our feelings have been understood. Someone heard the message behind the gift. We were saying, "I'm here for you," and the answer came, "I see that; I'm glad." We were noticed; we were thought of. Someone recognized our goodwill and trusted it, taking our outstretched hand. Between us was forged a living link of love.

Ingratitude has quite different effects. We give, we share, we serve, but nothing comes of it. Perhaps the gift itself is valued; the recipient may carry it off with glee and self-congratulation. But our desire to communicate, our will to enrich, has been ignored or quickly forgotten. The gift becomes for that other person an isolated thing. It conveys for him or her no gracious message; it creates no new bonds of relationship. Whatever love was in it falls to the ground unnoticed, unaccepted, apparently unwanted. The receiver has become merely a taker, a user. Whatever he may think of the gift, he thinks little of the giver. He's like the small girl who tears the wrapping off her birthday present and discards it, greeting card and all. The gift is her only interest. The question never occurs to her, "Who gave me this?"

When I think about these things, I wonder if I'm getting a glimpse of what human gratitude means to God. Apparently, it's what he wants from us more than anything else. To those who wonder about bringing him an acceptable offering, he recommends repeatedly the "sacrifice of thanksgiving." To render that, he declares, is truly to "honor" him (Ps. 50:23).

As gratitude is our most pleasing sacrifice, so unthankfulness tops the list of our sins. The apostle Paul can sum up the guilt and moral failure of the human race in these trenchant words: "...They are without excuse; for although they knew God, they did not honor him as God *or give thanks to him...*" (Rom. 1:20, 21, italics added). Everyone has enough light, he insists, to be thankful. At the root of all our other evils lies an astonishing, inexcusable want of gratitude.

Thankfulness, perhaps more than anything else, expresses the primal truth of our existence. We are *creatures.* We did not bring ourselves into being, but are dependent for life, breath, and all things on our Maker. Literally everything comes to us as a gift. We are never so truly human, so characteristically God's children, as when we are acknowledging that. Yes, and never so backward and perverse, never so evidently alienated from God, as when we show ourselves ungrateful.

And at that, the One who delights to give is grieved at heart. From all the gifts he has lavished on us, no relationship of trust and love has been formed. No grateful eyes look toward him, no words of thanks acknowledge him, no rising joy is shared. We tear the wrappings from each gift and make off with it, never seeming to wonder, *Who gave me this—and why?* No wonder Jesus asked with evident pain, when only one of the ten lepers he had healed returned to give thanks: "...Where are the nine?" (Luke 17:17).

Memory is the key to gratitude. Just as praise arises from "thinking magnificently" of God, so thanksgiving is stirred when we remember what he has given. Listen to the psalmist admonishing himself: "Bless the LORD, O my soul, and forget not all his benefits" (Ps. 103:2).

But that's the trick, isn't it, how not to forget? We have no lack in our time of "memory experts." Best-selling books promise to help us remember names (indispensable for politicians and clergymen), recall grocery lists, find misplaced objects, and retain most of what we read. But what can strengthen in us memory's highest function—calling to mind the mercies of God?

Christians often find that regular times for thanksgiving reinforce in them the spirit of gratitude. The more frequently and specifically we give thanks, the more capacity for appreciation we seem to develop. Building a definite time or times for thanksgiving into our daily schedules is perhaps the best corrective to our drift toward thoughtlessness, our common tendency to forget God.

Let there be planned moments at the close of each day when you recall the special mercies it has brought and say thanks. Let the common practice of thanking God for food at mealtimes carry over into your enjoyment of other daily gifts: the dawning light and the faces of loved ones (if you can see); the strength to be on your feet and go from place to place (if you can walk); the song of a bird or the voice of a friend (if you can hear).

But let memory range more widely. What a rich experience it is to look back over our lives, to savor again past mercies that still nourish and gladden us. It's a way of keeping in touch with life in its wholeness and continuity, and of sensing the love that has attended us along our way.

I like at times to thank God for the persons who have meant much to me, the special people in my life. I go back to ancestors like my great-great-grandfather Simeon Brownson, who wrote in his journal in 1834 about each day's family worship. "Thank you, Lord," I say, "for all my forebears who have feared you, all my family members who have served you, and for the blessing that flows down the generations from them to me and mine."

I was blessed with godly parents. I try not to let a day pass without thanking God for them, both now deceased. "Thank you, Father, for my mother and dad, for their trust in you, their love for each other, and all the affection, care, training, and affirmation they gave to me." I want to thank him for my sister, my grandparents, my aunts, and uncles.

Most precious of all, I have a dear wife and four fine sons (one already in heaven). We rejoice in two lovely daughters-in-law, and (at present count) six incomparable grandchildren. "Lord, don't let a day go by in which I forget to thank you for them!"

"Thank you, Lord, for good friends and fellow laborers. Thank you for all who have somehow served me, taught me, prayed for me, encouraged me, believed in me, put up with me, or cleaned up after me." Where would I be, who would I be, without them?

Do you know what it does for us when we thank God for other people? Marvelous things. We see them through new eyes. We're helped not to stereotype them, to presume that we have them all figured out. We get a glimpse of the depth and richness of who they are, and begin to appreciate them all the more. We find ourselves focusing on their graces instead of their foibles, or at least seeing those foibles with more grace!

Thanksgiving preserves our sense of wonder, doesn't it? When we thank God for the bread we eat and the water we drink, for breath in our lungs and the ceaseless beat of our hearts, none of that seems commonplace any more. The sheer miracle of being alive breaks in on us afresh. Everything takes on a dimension of depth. Ordinary things are strangely new.

Thankful people are always the happiest ones. Pity the men, the women, who see no one to thank. Life for them is bleak and joyless. They have nothing to celebrate but their own luck. There's no Giver to appreciate, no thoughtful love to savor. It's "just the way the ball bounces." No big deal. But when we thank the Lord, our cup is always full and spilling over.

I remember visiting in the homes of Chol Indians once, down in Chiapas, Mexico. These people, beyond the bare necessities, had almost nothing. They lived in tiny huts with dirt floors. But they were radiant. Their faces shone with an irrepressible joy. They had recently embraced the Christian faith, and seemed overcome with thankfulness.

They reminded me of a lady I used to visit frequently in my first pastorate. Mrs. Terhune, when I knew her, had lost by death six of her seven children: one at two years, one at three, one at twelve, one at thirteen, one at twenty-eight, and one at fifty-two. She had been through major surgery on four different occasions. As a young, in-experienced pastor, with scant knowledge of the tragic, I was stunned at her story. How could she endure all that? How could she remain so cheerful? How could she say (as she did on several occasions) "I don't know how I could have gotten through it if the Lord hadn't been with me"? She couldn't thank him enough.

I'm not recommending thankfulness because it will make you happy, childlike and zestful about life. We ought to thank God because he is gracious, and do it every day because his gifts keep coming. But if you're going to be consistently thankful, you'd better prepare for gladness. It will come. Those who take on thanksgiving bravely as a duty can't escape invasions of delight. "It is good"—in many ways—"to give thanks to the LORD!" (Ps. 92:1).

For Response and Resolve

Let me not forget God's mercies to me, but let me offer them back to him each day in thanksgiving.

For Reading and Meditation

> Psalm 103:1–5
> Psalm 116:12–17
> Luke 17:11–19
> Colossians 3:12–17

For Reflection and Discussion

1. Why are we hurt by the ingratitude of others?
2. How is gratitude related to faith?

3. Why do you suppose our thankfulness is valued by God?

4. What most stimulates gratitude in you?

5. What happens in our lives as we grow more and more thankful?

7

The Call to Confession
Agreeing with God

I said, "I will confess my transgressions to the Lord"; then thou didst forgive the guilt of my sin (Ps. 32:5).

Because, if you confess with your lips that Jesus is Lord and believe in your heart that God raised him from the dead, you will be saved. For man believes with his heart and so is justified, and he confesses with his lips and so is saved (Rom. 10:9, 10).

Depression comes, not from having faults, but from the refusal to face them. There are tens of thousands of persons today, suffering from fears which in reality are nothing but the effects of hidden sins.

Fulton J. Sheen

What does it mean to *confess?* Most of us link that word with "owning up" to a wrong, admitting a fault, accepting responsibility for what we have done. "Come on now," say the authorities to the cowering suspect, "We know you're guilty. Confess!"

It often has that precise meaning in the Bible. Listen to this psalm of David:

I acknowledged my sin to thee
and I did not hide my iniquity;

> I said, "I will confess my transgressions to the LORD";
> then thou didst forgive the guilt of my sin (Ps. 32:5).

Here "confessing our transgressions" is clearly contrasted with "hiding our iniquity." To confess is to "come clean," to acknowledge to God both our sinfulness and our particular sins.

We find the same emphasis in the New Testament. The apostle John writes to his friends that "If we confess our sins, he is faithful and just and will forgive us our sins and to cleanse us from all unrighteousness" (1 John 1:9). Once again, confession is contrasted with concealment, with refusal to admit guilt. "If we say we have no sin, we deceive ourselves and the truth is not in us" (v. 8). To deny our blameworthiness, says John, is to remain in the darkness (v. 6). To acknowledge the truth about ourselves is to "walk in the light" (v. 7).

In the Greek language, to confess means, literally, "to speak the same as" or to "agree with." When we confess our sins to God, we take his view of them, call them what he calls them, affirm his verdict about us as true. "If," on the other hand, "we say we have not sinned," says John, we make God "a liar, and his word is not in us" (v. 10). In that case we're saying, "No, Lord, I don't agree with your estimate of my actions, your weighing of my motives. You and I see these things differently."

When we insist on disagreeing with God, rejecting his word about us, we become more and more alienated from him. Refusal to confess our sins is a retreat from his presence—a spurning of his light. In seeking to prove ourselves "in the right," we must make him out as "in the wrong."

We even become alienated from ourselves. When I confront the truth about myself and refuse to accept it, I sacrifice my integrity. I become divided against myself. Guilt, when repressed, begins to destroy me from within.

Hear David lamenting his lot when he had attempted to hide his great wrong against Uriah and Bathsheba:

> When I declared not my sin, my body wasted away
>   through my groaning all day long.
> For day and night thy hand was heavy upon me;
>   my strength was dried up as by the heat of summer
>   (Ps. 32:3, 4).

The concealment made him physically ill. He felt himself under fearful pressure. All his vital energies withered away as though scorched by the desert sun. He was profoundly miserable.

Who of us hasn't felt that way at times? We know we've acted shamefully, but we won't admit it. We clutch a guilty secret to our breasts until it eats away at us. Unable to bear the pain of that inner judgment, we begin to project blame onto others. We become defensive, bitter perhaps, harshly critical. Hating ourselves, we spew hostility in all directions. Everything wearies us, and we find no rest.

What a difference it makes when we confess! David tells about it:

> ...I said, "I will confess my transgressions to the LORD";
>   then thou didst forgive the guilt of my sin....
> Blessed is he whose transgression is forgiven,
>   whose sin is covered.
> Blessed is the man to whom the
> LORD imputes no iniquity... (32:5, 1, 2).

How great it is, he's saying, to get all that off my chest, and taste the joy of God's pardon! What a burden lifted! What a misery ended!

Sometimes we think of confession as though it were merely an initiation into the Christian life, a once-for-all act. But John was writing to believers when he commended confession so highly. Jesus taught his disciples to pray regularly, "Forgive us our debts, as we forgive our debtors" (Matt. 6:12).

On the last night he was with them, our Lord showed his disciples by a moving parable their need of his ever-fresh cleansing. Remember when he was washing the feet of his disciples and Peter objected, "You shall never wash my feet" (John 13:8)? Jesus' reply was, "If I do not wash you, you have no part in me" (v. 8). We cannot belong to him, apparently, without opening ourselves again and again to his cleansing touch.

Not that we must become Christians all over again every time we sin. Poor Peter, after our Lord's warning, craved a total washing: "Lord, not my feet only, but also my hands and my head!" (v. 9). But that wasn't necessary. "He who has bathed does not need to wash except for his feet..." (v. 10), replies Jesus. God grants a total cleansing, a full acceptance to all who receive Christ by faith. That need not be repeated. But in their daily walk of life, even the most devoted of disciples contract defilement. We all need in that sense to have "our feet washed" day by day. As John Calvin once put it, "Christ always finds in us something to cleanse."

What does a daily confession of sin to God actually accomplish? Obviously it provides for the Almighty no new insight! He is the heart-searcher, who knows us far better than we know ourselves. Our acknowledgments of guilt and wrong can hardly be for his benefit.

Nor do they secure his favor, as though atoning in some way for our misdeeds. Christ has died for those sins, once and for all. Our pardon, our acceptance, our new standing with God, rest completely on his finished work. Confession does not—cannot—add anything to that. But it does open the way for us to appropriate—and enjoy—God's forgiving mercy.

As we confess our sins, we leave behind our hiding and pretending. We learn to be honest. We come out of the shadows into God's dazzling light. And there, trembling, vulnerable, we make a cheering discovery. The light that exposes also heals. Life for us is suddenly clean and new again. We have communion with God and with one another. We go on our way rejoicing. Prayer and praise leap up freely from our hearts. How wonderful it is to be forgiven!

When should we confess our sins to God? In one sense the answer is obvious: when we first become aware of them. Our tendency, however, is all the other way. We put off the moment of honest admission, don't we? We may be vaguely conscious of some wrong in our lives, but we are reluctant to face it squarely. We are uneasy, troubled, but it still seems hard to label what we've done, to turn toward God and acknowledge it. Maybe we think that stewing in our guiltiness for a while is a kind of penance. We'll suffer first for our sins, and confess them later!

A friend of mine used to describe a "clean person" in this way: "A clean person tries not to get dirty. When he does get dirty, as all of us do, he tries to get cleaned up again as soon as possible." Christians, at their best, are like that. They don't want to sin; they seek to avoid every kind of evil. But when they do stumble and fall they don't just lie there in the mud of their failure. They get up again, confess to God, accept his cleansing, and go on their way.

There is absolutely nothing to be gained by delaying our confession. That only prolongs our misery and saps our productivity. Further, fretting over unconfessed sin is make-believe repentance. For us to grovel in guilt feelings does God no honor. We give glory to him when we confess our transgressions and depend wholly on Christ to save us from them.

Many Christians find it helpful also to set aside a specific time each day for confession of their sins. They remember that Jesus taught his followers to pray "forgive us our debts" as often as they pray "give us this day our daily bread." They open themselves each day to the cleansing light of God's Word and Spirit. They ask:

> Search me, O God, and know my heart.
> Try me and know my thoughts.
> And see if there be any wicked way in me,
> and lead me in the way everlasting (Ps. 139:23, 24).

If you are inclined to do that, here's a suggestion: find a time during the day when you are most alert and when your conscience is most sensitive. Some Christians confess their sins in the evening, before they retire for the night. That doesn't work for me. I'm too sleepy then. More than that, I'm too obtuse.

I'm a morning person. I do better at almost anything in the early part of the day. As the hours wear on, I seem to become less effective, less agreeable. The evening is the time of day when I become most vulnerable to ill moods and most likely to treat others unkindly. And the worst thing is, I seem to feel justified in acting that way. I've sometimes said nasty things to my family members at night—with scarcely a twinge of conscience. I was sure that I was right. What I was expressing was only the indignation of the righteous.

But by the next morning, everything looked different to me—drastically different. What I had viewed so smugly the night before seemed shabby and heartless now. How could I say such a thing to one I love? I've often had to confess such wrongs to the Lord in my morning prayers and then apologize to the one I had hurt. The morning has been for me a time of inner moral awakening. Again and again, the early hours have been my best for self-examination and confession.

But frank acknowledgment of sin is not the only form of confession. It's not the only way in which we "agree with God," or "speak the same" as he does. Christians are also to confess their *faith*. They are to confess Jesus as Lord. They are to speak with gladness of the salvation they receive through him.

We usually think of that confession as public, before our fellow Christians, or especially before an unbelieving world. When Jesus speaks to his followers about "confessing" or "denying" him "before men," he pictures a situation of conflict, where the truth is on trial. In the crisis we either confess or deny him; we claim or disown him; we identify ourselves with him and his cause or we say in effect, "I do not know the man."

But the term *confess* is also used to describe Jesus at prayer. He gives praise and thanks to the Father, and affirms the truth before him:

> At that time, Jesus confessed, "I thank thee, Father, Lord of heaven and earth, that thou hast hid these things from the wise and understanding, and hast revealed them to babes" (Matt. 11:25).

This is for our Lord a confession—a confession of faith. Here confession means giving voice to our most cherished convictions, affirming what we know to be true, reciting our personal creed.

When I quote the twenty-third Psalm: "The Lord is my shepherd…" I am praying. At one point I say to the Lord, "I will fear no evil, for thou art with me. Thy rod and thy staff, they comfort me…." But the prayer is also an affirmation, a confession of all the Lord is to me.

I've become convinced in recent years that this is a vitally important kind of praying. Think, for example, about what we call our "self-image." We're being told on every hand how important for our mental health, our relationships with others, our happiness and success in life is the way we look at ourselves. Further, we learn that much of what we believe about ourselves has been programmed into us by family members, by others special to us. Some influential person in your past teased you about being ugly or homely, and you believed him. A teacher said you were "slow," and you hung your head. A frustrated, anxious parent predicted that you would never amount to anything, or someone screamed at you that you were a liar and couldn't be trusted. Messages like that—and more positive ones as well—are affecting you profoundly today, still shaping your self-image.

If we encounter people who love us, who show us "unconditional positive regard," many of those negative self-feelings can change. These caring ones believe in us. They affirm us. They tell us that we are significant persons. We are "somebody special," and we begin to think about ourselves in a new way. We see ourselves through the eyes of those who love us.

That happens supremely when we come to know God in Jesus Christ. We were afraid that we didn't matter, but he tells us we were made in his image. We thought no one really cared about us, but he loved us enough to die for us, and he claims us as his own. Faith means seeing ourselves from his perspective and saying about ourselves what he says.

So don't stop with confessing that you are a sinner. That's true, but it's only a part of what's true about you, and not even the most significant part. If you have trusted in Jesus Christ, God says of you that you are a man or woman, girl or boy, "in Christ." Try affirming that in his presence day by day. "I am in Christ. I am a member of his body. I am joined to the unseen Lord."

God says that in Christ you are totally forgiven. You are completely and forever accepted. You are welcomed. Say your "Amen" to that. Affirm it as true. "I am loved. I belong."

God says that in Christ you have died to the mastery of sin and Satan, and have been raised again to live for a new Master. You have been resurrected to walk in new-ness of life. Take your stand on that. "I am free. I can live for the One who died for me." Proclaim that to be true in spite of all your weaknesses, all your up-and-down strug-gles, all the accusations of the Evil One.

God says that his Holy Spirit has been given to renew your whole being, to strengthen and guide you. Accept the truth of that. Say that it's so. Honor the Spirit as dwelling within you, making your body his temple.

God says that you are gifted, that you have a work to do, a ministry to exercise, a significant contribution to make. Agree with him. Confess that before him. Refuse to tolerate demeaning, self-belittling thoughts. Keep saying about yourself what he says.

Now that is not a kind of self-hypnosis. It's not a device to "psych yourself up"—to make you believe something that isn't so. God's Word about you, remember, is the *truth*. To plant your feet on it, to affirm it as true, is to base your life on the ultimate Reality.

The result, therefore, is more than a psychological adjustment. When you affirm God's truth, you open yourself to his transforming power. To say *Amen* to his promise is to exercise genuine *faith*.

Think of God's Word as like "the Promised Land," like the milk-and-honey country that lay before Israel's leader, Joshua. God had given it to Joshua, but that wasn't an invitation to sit passively, to take the inheri-tance for granted. He was to march into the land and appropriate it. The promise of God was, "Every place that the sole of your foot will tread upon have I given to you..." (Josh. 1:3). And today his promises, his words of grace and salvation, are given to *you*. March in and claim them. Whatever the struggle, however fierce the opposi-tion, affirm the promises to be yours in Jesus Christ. You have the faith. God has given it to you. Now confess it, and find the power to live accordingly!

I want to talk with you in the next chapter about *commitment*—about yielding your life to Christ as Lord. But in a sense, what we're looking at now comes first. Before you can make a commitment, you need to know who you are. You need to have a significant self to give away. God tells you in his Word who you are. Say to him each day, "Yes, Lord, that's who I am in Jesus Christ. And here, I offer myself to you."

I hope that through all your life you will be a *confessor* in this twofold way: "I am a sinner, but I am also one of God's chosen ones. I am guilty, yet forgiven; without excuse, but justified. I am a son [or daughter] of disobedience, but by God's grace I'm a child of the living God. In myself I am lost, but in Christ, I am redeemed."

That double confession, that double awareness, will keep us both honest and optimistic, humble and grateful, penitent and triumphantly glad. When we so confess, we renounce all trust in ourselves and rest completely on God's mercy and faithfulness. In faith we say, "Not to us, O LORD, not to us, but to thy name give glory..." (Ps. 115:1).

For Response and Resolve

Trusting in God's saving grace, let me each day make confession of my sins and of my salvation in Christ.

For Reading and Meditation

Psalm 23
Psalm 32:1–7
Proverbs 28:13, 14
Romans 10:9–13
1 John 1:5–10

For Reflection and Discussion

1. Since God is all-knowing, why do we need to confess our sins?

2. Why is confession so often accompanied by joy and relief?

3. When should we confess?

4. Why is it important to affirm, to confess, what God says about us? How can we do that regularly?

8

The Call to Commitment
Offering Ourselves

And he said to all, "If any man would come after me, let him deny himself and take up his cross daily and follow me" (Luke 9:23).

I appeal to you therefore, brethren, by the mercies of God, to present your bodies as a living sacrifice, holy and acceptable to God, which is your spiritual worship (Rom. 12:1).

We become persons only by making a personal decision.

Paul Tournier

You are invited to commit yourself to the Lord each day in your prayers. Remember how he said to his disciples, "If any man would come after me, let him deny himself and take up his cross daily and follow me" (Luke 9:23)?

This was an invitation. He did not *order* them to come along. There was no pressure, no demand. Jesus would neither wheedle or manipulate. *If any man will,* he said, *if anyone really wants to, then. . . .* The choice was up to them. It was clear that he wanted them to come. He had chosen them long before, sought them out, invited each to join him. But now, at a new crossroads, they were still free to choose. They were invited again—invited to make a fresh commitment.

The commitment was to "come after" him. He had told them that he was headed for Jerusalem, and for trouble. "...the Son of man must suffer many things, and be rejected by the elders and chief priests and scribes, and be killed, and after three days rise again" (Mark 8:31). In the light of that, would they stay with him? Would they face the consequences of being identified with him? Would each shoulder his cross, as though on the way to die with him?

Apparently the decision had to be made over and over again. Discipleship was begun decisively, but never settled once for all. The followers of Jesus still had other options available. They could say no to him: they could join the disenchanted ones who had drifted away. Each morning the invitation came afresh. *If anyone wants to come after me, let him say no to himself, and take up his cross daily.* In other words, let him commit himself *today.*

How does that apply to people like us? We aren't walking with the Lord in Galilee, as these men were. Jesus of Nazareth doesn't point us down a road that leads to Jerusalem and ask if we want to follow him there. But, does he call us also in some way to commitment, to daily decision?

Paul thought so. When the great apostle sent his letter to the church in Rome, he knew he was writing to believers. These people had made a commitment in repentance and faith to Christ as Lord. They had chosen to follow the risen Jesus. But after reminding them about the riches of the gospel, Paul calls them to give themselves afresh: "I appeal to you therefore, brethren, by the mercies of God, to present your bodies as a living sacrifice, holy and acceptable to God, which is your spiritual worship" (Rom. 12:1).

Note again that this is an invitation. Paul echoes his Master. He is not ordering here, but appealing; not barking commands at people, but warmly beseeching them. His only leverage is "the mercies of God," the grace they have freely received. Nothing is forced on these Roman disciples. They are invited to offer themselves freely.

Paul uses here the imagery of Old Testament sacrifice. In the worship of Israel, burnt offerings were designed to express the total self-dedication of the people. In this form of sacrifice, an entire animal was placed on the altar to be consumed by fire.

In the spiritual worship of "the new Israel," the church of Jesus Christ, animal sacrifice is no more. Now Christians present to God not the bodies of sacrificial animals, but their own bodies—their whole selves. This is not the sacrifice of the dead but of those newly alive. All these offerings are pleasing to God, says Paul, acceptable to him, through the one perfect sacrifice of Christ.

But there is more to the image. The burnt offering was distinguished from other sacrifices because it was *continual*. In the worship of the sanctuary, the fire on the altar was never to go out. Each morning the priests would scrape away the ashes of what had been burned and place on the remaining embers a new offering. The self-commitment of the worshipers was not only to be entire and all-consuming; it was to be renewed each day. For all who want to follow Jesus, in whatever age, there is a spiritual worship to be offered, an entire self-surrender to be made—every day.

Why, we wonder, should such repeated expressions of commitment be called for? Isn't one sincere act of self-dedication enough? I had a friend in seminary who told some of us frequently, "I consecrated my life to the Lord fourteen years ago." If he did that, and meant it, what more was needed?

Apparently Peter needed more. Few would question his sincerity when he first clambered out of his fishing boat to go with the Lord. He left everything to follow. He later confessed joyfully that Jesus was the Christ, the Son of God. But after the resurrection, when Peter was wondering what would become of his fellow disciple John, the risen Lord brought him up short. "...what is that to you? Follow me" (John 21:22). It was the same call Peter had heard long before by the seaside. Now he needed to hear it again. He needed to get back on track. He needed to decide once more that he would concentrate on following Jesus.

What was wrong with Peter? The same thing that is wrong with you and me. He was sincere when he set out to walk with Jesus, but he didn't realize all that would be involved. Further, he didn't know how weak and unstable he was. He never dreamed he could become for a time the devil's mouthpiece. (Remember in Matthew 16:23 how Jesus had to say to him, "Get behind me, Satan! You are a hindrance to me; for you are not on the side of God, but of men"?) Peter refused to believe that he could play the coward and deny his master. He had turned to the Lord once, but later he was told that he would need to be "converted" again (*see* Luke 22:32).

Like Peter, we really mean it when we turn our lives over to Christ. With all our hearts, we want to follow him. But most of us have little awareness at the time of what that commitment will entail. An eight-year-old boy, I'm convinced, can decide sincerely to follow Jesus. He surrenders all he knows of himself to the Lord. But what he knows is not very extensive! He can't foresee, for example, what passing through puberty will mean, what new energies and drives will soon be released in him. He can't even imagine the challenging decisions he will need to make as a teenager if he seriously intends to live as a Christian.

When a young girl becomes a believer, can she possibly envision the pressures she will face in deciding about marriage and career? Does a young man coming to Christ know how much he's affected by personal ambition? Do any of us see how vulnerable we are to the yen for possessions or the craving for power? Do we realize how insatiably hungry we are for affirmation from others? Who of us can anticipate the sorrows and hard choices that may accompany our discipleship?

The Spanish thinker Miguel Unamuno once wrote that the moment a person takes up the attitude of commitment, he or she is headed for an experience of suffering and a firsthand knowledge of the tragic. Didn't Jesus warn his followers of that in John 16:33: "In the world you shall have tribulation"? Each fork in the road, each new trial in life raises afresh the question of commitment. We have to decide again: Will Christ be my Lord in this decision, in this dark valley, in this new dimension of experience?

It isn't simply that changing scenes and circumstances make us reevaluate our commitment. *We* are the problem. We have great difficulty in remaining committed to Christ. We give ourselves away to him, but all too readily we "take ourselves back." The resistance within us to going God's way is amazingly stubborn and persistent. We don't conquer it overnight. It keeps cropping up again in unexpected, embarrassing ways. Overcoming it seems to require not a single stroke but a prolonged siege. The life of a disciple involves repeated decisions, ever-renewed turning toward the Lord.

If we are married persons, how do we remain committed to our spouses? Does one moment of self-pledging do it for a lifetime? When we say in our marriage vows, "I do...I will..." does that settle the issue? Hardly. Thousands of people who once recited those vows sincerely have since forgotten or renounced them. Commitment to another person, if it is to be strong and enduring, needs repeated expressions. It isn't enough to say at the outset,

"I love you," and expect your spouse to remember that for fifty years! There is an ingenuity about caring. It's always devising new ways to show itself, new channels in which to find expression. In real commitment, you choose your spouse today, just as you did on your wedding day. You speak your love, and then you speak it again. Your partner needs to hear that, and you—every bit as much—need to say it.

Words are not the only ways in which we pledge ourselves. Words are meager and disappointing if they are alone—if there are no acts of love to reinforce them. But, oh, what words can sometimes do! Life and death are in the power of the tongue. Words can kill and make alive. They can sometimes even bring deeds along with them, and kindle a dying flame of devotion.

You are invited to commit yourself daily to Jesus Christ—in prayer. God says to his people, "Take with you words and return to the LORD..." (Hos. 14:2). Let your self-offering to God be the decision of your whole being, and then let it find expression in your praying. This, as the apostle says, is your *spiritual worship.* You bring it not with hands but with heart and voice. Tell the Lord that this day you are choosing to deny yourself and take up your cross and follow him. Tell him that you are offering, gladly and gratefully, your whole self in worship. Yield up to him your members to be his instruments, his weapons of righteousness. Maybe on some days you'll want to name one by one the aspects of your life that you commit to him.

> Here, Lord, I offer you all my energies and abilities. Here is my physical life and health for you to keep and use. Here is my mind for you to illumine. Here are my emotions for you to release, to purify and order. Here is my will for you to govern. Here is all I possess, that you may guide me in my stewardship. Here, Lord, is my heart, my work, my way. I give myself entirely to you.

Do you think God will be pleased if you so offer yourself to him each day? The apostle Paul says that he will, that all such "spiritual worship," such "living sacrifices" (Rom. 12:1) are acceptable to him through Christ. He delights in them. He invites you to bring them.

Do you think that doing this daily will make a difference in the way you live? Try it and see. It may be that just as words of endearment to a spouse can lead you to act toward him or her more kindly, so your prayers of commitment will help you to lead a dedicated life. Paul teaches that when we yield ourselves to God, for him to renew and transform us, we can more and more discern his will and do it (*see* v. 2). We can increasingly use our gifts not for self-display but in the service of others. We can follow Jesus in growing, deepening commitment.

Charles Whiston, in his rich book *Pray: A Study of Distinctive Christian Praying,* tells of a commitment prayer he prays each morning:

> O Lord Jesus Christ:
> In obedience to thy holy claim upon me,
> I give myself anew to thee this day;
> all that I am,
> all that I have;
> to be wholly and unconditionally thine for thy using.

What especially impressed me as I read this prayer was the author's way of preparing for it. Just after waking, before getting out of bed, he imagines Christ saying to him,

> I am your Lord Jesus Christ
> I was the agent of my Father in creating you;
> I died upon the cross for you.
> Therefore, you do not belong to yourself;
> You belong to me.
> Will you give yourself to me this day?

98 Courage to Pray

Then comes the prayer of commitment. Isn't that a marvelous way to pray? We listen, then speak. We hear the Word of grace, then offer ourselves in gratitude. That's what Paul meant when he wrote, "I appeal to you, therefore, brethren, by the mercies of God, to present your bodies..." (Rom. 12:1). Our commitment is always in response to his claim. First his saving love; then our self-giving. Everything starts with "the mercies of God."

Whiston describes these words of morning commitment as his "Snowflake Prayer." A snowflake, as you know, is exquisite but fragile. You marvel at its intricate beauty, but if you hold it in your hand or breathe on it, it disappears. But in the winter, over mountainous areas, billions of snowflakes descend. They build up on mountain slopes to depths of thirty feet or more. The snow settles under its own weight, hardens, and turns to ice. During alternate periods of melting and freezing, chunks of rock become embedded in the mass. When the glacier begins to move, it can wear away solid granite and send it down the slopes as so much sand.

Like the snowflake, one prayer of commitment is both impressive and delicate. But through prayers that accumulate, through daily decisions to follow, through fresh self-offerings to the Lord, Whiston sees a buildup of weight and power. We find God eroding the granite hardness of our hearts as we become more completely his.

One impulse of the heart to follow may not hold. We may become distracted, diverted. But as we set our hearts day after day, we begin to establish a fixed direction for our lives and keep moving toward God and his purpose for us. Let there fall today one more snowflake of commitment!

For Response and Resolve

In response to his saving grace, let me offer to God afresh each day all that I am and have.

For Reading and Meditation

Leviticus 6:8–13
Luke 9:23, 24; 14:25–33
Romans 6:12–14; 12:1, 2
1 Peter 2:1–5

For Reflection and Discussion

1. In what sense is our commitment to Christ a *response*?
2. Why does our commitment need to be renewed?
3. How are "words" of commitment related to "lives" of commitment?
4. How will you seek to renew your commitment to Christ today?

9

The Call to Petition
Asking for Good Gifts

Ask, and it will be given you; seek, and you will find; knock, and it will be opened to you. For every one who asks receives, and he who seeks finds, and to him who knocks it will be opened. Or what man of you, if his son asks him for bread, will give him a stone? Or if he asks for a fish, will give him a serpent? If you then, who are evil, know how to give good gifts to your children, how much more will your Father who is in heaven give good things to those who ask him! (Matt. 7:7–11).

Prayer is a sincere, sensible, affectionate pouring out of the soul to God, through Christ, in the strength and assistance of the Spirit, for such things as God has promised.

John Bunyan

You are invited to ask the Father for "good things." That's right. He wants you to have them. And he wants you to *ask.*

Many people seem to have trouble believing that. They aren't sure it's a good idea to make requests of God. They feel uncomfortable asking for his gifts. They wonder if he really wants them to do that, if he approves of such petitions.

Some teachers on the subject of prayer contribute to that uneasiness. I can remember reading books and hearing sermons on prayer which have pointedly raised such questions. If you took them seriously, you would tend to feel squeamish about asking God for anything, especially for yourself. Here's the gist of what they say: "When you come to God, you shouldn't haul out your 'shopping list.' Your prayer shouldn't be, 'Give me this' and 'Give me that.'"

We know what they mean. The idea (a good one!) behind those words is that we ought to be concerned about praising God, enjoying fellowship with him, and doing his will. But the clear implication is that petitions for his gifts are less fitting, less genuinely religious, than these other forms of prayer.

In such presentations, asking is usually acknowledged to have some place in prayer. But that seems almost reluctantly allowed. Petition is treated as an elementary form of prayer, presumably for those who are still childish and immature. The more advanced in the spiritual life are thought to move beyond it, to rise above the asking stage. Some even contend that the ideal of prayer, the height of spiritual attainment, would not include petition at all, but only wordless contemplation.

Now that line of teaching has a certain plausibility in it. Most of us who pray are conscious of having made our share of petty and selfish requests. We're keenly aware that praise to God and communion with him should have a larger place in our praying. As a result, we may feel vulnerable to criticisms about our prayers of asking.

But when we downplay petition, we are veering away from Jesus' central teaching about prayer. Take, for example, these familiar words from the Sermon on the Mount:

Ask, and it will be given you; seek, and you will find; knock, and it will be opened to you. For every one who asks receives, and he who seeks finds, and to him who knocks it will be opened. Or what man of you, if his son

asks him for bread, will give him a stone? Or if he asks for
a fish, will give him a serpent? If you then, who are evil,
know how to give good gifts to your children, how much
more will your Father who is in heaven give good things to
those who ask him! (Matt. 7:7–11).

Did you notice how much Jesus said here about asking? In the space of a few verses, he uses the verb *ask* or
one of its synonyms nine times! This profound lesson of
Jesus on prayer is *all* about asking.

Or think of that marvelous pattern for our praying
which we call *The Lord's Prayer.* After its opening address to God as Father, it consists almost entirely of
petitions: in Luke's version of it, five of them; in Matthew's, six. For Jesus, whose whole life was praise to the
Father, communion with him and submission to his will,
the heart of prayer was still *asking.*

The point is so obvious that it's remarkable anyone
could miss it. The word *prayer* with us has come to have
a broad connotation. But the original verb *to pray,* in
Hebrew, in Greek, and in every language into which the
Bible is translated, means essentially *to make request, to
ask.* Asking is not a preliminary phase, not a stepping-
stone to better things, but the main substance of biblical
prayer. If we insist on calling it juvenile, it's good to
remember that our Lord told the sophisticates of his day
that they needed to become as little children to enter
his kingdom!

"But," someone objects, "we might ask for something
contrary to God's will." That's right; we might. Moses
did. He asked God to allow him to enter the Promised
Land, but God said no. Paul did. He wanted that thorn in
the flesh to be removed, but the Lord said, "My grace is
sufficient for you..." (2 Cor. 12:9). Even Jesus did!
He prayed in Gethsemane, "...let this cup pass from
me..." (Matt. 26:39). But that was not to be. He had to
drain it to the bitter dregs.

God will deal with our requests in his infinite wisdom and love, no matter how short-sighted or how foolish they may be. The fear that we may ask for something wrongly is self-engendered. God doesn't impose such scruples. He says in his dear Son, "Come, ask what you will. Seek and knock freely." We can pour out our hearts before him as beloved children to a listening Father. He delights in that.

Becoming a Christian, learning to know God through Christ, begins with asking. The gift is freely offered; the great work of redemption has been fully done. Now it is for us to pray the prayer of receptive faith, "...God be merciful to me, a sinner..." (Luke 18:13). "Jesus, remember me when you come into your kingly power" (23:42). "...Save, Lord; we are perishing" (Matt. 8:25). He holds out to you and me the cup of salvation. He offers forgiveness and new life. Ask. Ask today. Ask now, and it shall be given you.

Then begins a life in which you continue spreading all your concerns before his throne. Don't leave asking behind. Don't imagine that you'll ever reach a point where a cry of need will be inappropriate. Maturity in the life of faith surely doesn't mean independence and self-sufficiency. It means rather becoming more childlike, more simple in trust, more conscious of our need and his grace. It may be that what many of us need most of all is to learn again how to ask.

In calling us to pray, Jesus also promises that our asking, seeking, and knocking will surely be answered. "Ask, and it shall be given you; seek, and you will find; knock, and it will be opened to you..." (Matt. 7:7ff.). Then he goes over the same ground again. "Every one who asks receives." No exceptions to that, apparently. "He who seeks finds...to him who knocks it will be opened." Let that sink in for a moment. Let the assurance of it take deep root. Our approaches and appeals to God, our sighs and searchings after him, our petitions and pleas will *never* be in vain. No situation about which we pray will ever remain the same. In every case, a gift will be given us. Something will reveal itself to us. Some door will surely open.

Here is another point in which some contemporary treatments of prayer may mislead us badly. Prayer, we are told, is meant to have effect, not on God, but on ourselves. By praying we gain psychological release. We discover new ways of dealing with our problems or we learn to adjust better to our circumstances. In this view prayer is getting in touch with your own resources, "psyching yourself up." Or, as someone once described it to me, it is "dipping into your little pool of ego-strength."

Now I don't mean to disparage the inward effects of prayer. They are considerable. I know of nothing that so promotes mental wholeness as earnest praying. But for Jesus, prayer has such staggering power—not because it is a handy means for self-improvement—but because God acts in response to it—doing things that would not otherwise be done. He is the God who works in our circumstances as well as in our hearts, when we ask and seek and knock.

Friends, this is the lifeblood of genuine faith. This is what keeps people praying. Prayer seen as auto-suggestion may be tried as a technique, but it will never be the heart's occupation, the strenuous activity of a lifetime. We leave off praying with persistence and passion when we stop believing it makes a difference, when we lose sight of the One who unfailingly responds to it.

As I've been thinking about this chapter for the last few weeks, I've asked myself the question, "Why do I believe that? Why have I been banking on it since I first met Christ over forty years ago?" Is it because I've seen it work every time, because I've always been able to identify God's answer to my prayer? No, that's not it. I've seen that vividly sometimes—but not always.

In fact, I've been many times baffled, totally unable to figure things out. It seemed that my prayers and those of others were not being answered at all. Time dragged on and nothing happened. Any thought I had entertained of being a "prayer expert" was simply blown away.

I believe this word, "Ask, and you shall receive" because Jesus said it. Because *Jesus* said it. He is the Son of the Father. He knows about the ways of God with us and he is altogether true. Christians call him "the faithful witness." His whole life had the ring of truth about it. He never led anyone astray. I take this word about our asking and God's answering on his authority.

And it wasn't only that he *said* it. His obedient life, his death on a cross for us and his resurrection have all *confirmed* it. Now I have to agree with the apostle Paul's irresistible logic: "If God is for us, who is against us? He who did not spare his own Son but gave him up for us all, will he not also give us all things with him?" (Rom. 8:31, 32). Yes, if he gave us—unasked—the greatest gift of all, he will *never* send us away empty when we call on him in need.

What I especially want to think about with you now is how these gifts which God bestows in answer to our prayers are *good*. Jesus promises that the Father will give eminently helpful gifts. He won't mock us with worthless or harmful substitutes, a stone for bread, or a scorpion instead of an egg. No, God will give what we really need, what corresponds to our true wants, what our whole being cries out for.

What are the good gifts? We don't always know, do we? Sometimes it seems that we're learning all our lifetime what "good gifts" really are. Some of the things we once saw as supremely desirable haven't turned out to be so satisfying.

Take a moment now to think about "good things." What do you suppose would be the best gifts God could give you? What would you prize most highly? What would make you happiest if you could receive it? What would benefit you most? If you could have your "druthers," what would be your fondest wish, your heart's desire?

Try not to answer too quickly. Sometimes the things that come to our minds first aren't the deepest in us. They excite us, but when we reflect about them, we realize that having them wouldn't make much difference to us, wouldn't change our lives appreciably for the better. There are other things that, down deep, we may want more.

I may have an advantage on you here, because I've been thinking about this question for some time. I've had opportunity to prune and revise my "list." I think I'm learning what I want most, what for me the best gifts are. For some of them, I've been asking for a good many years.

Near the top of the list for me is this: "Create in me a clean heart, O God, and put a new and right spirit within me" (Ps. 51:10). Jesus taught that all our speaking and living proceeds from the "heart" (*see* Mark 7:20–23). "From it," says the proverb, "flow the streams of life" (Prov. 4:23). If God will create in me each day a new kind of heart, and give me a "right spirit," then everything else in my life will surely be affected for the better. Now there's a good gift!

Here's another like it: "...teach me wisdom in my secret heart" (Ps. 51:6). According to the psalms and proverbs, the chief part of wisdom is "the fear of the LORD." What if God were to implant within us such wisdom that the fear of the Lord would be in our consciousness all day long, that we would be aware of living under his eye? Wouldn't that be something? What a gift—to be inwardly aware all the time that God is real and he is *there!*

The apostle Paul once expressed this desire: "…Christ will be honored in my body, whether by life or by death" (Phil. 1:20). Whatever happened to him, Paul wanted Jesus to be revealed, to be seen as great and glorious, in his life. That possibility draws me too. I want to say, "Lord, let it be so!"

Jesus told his followers that if they would believe in him, "rivers of living water" would pour out from within them (*see* John 7:37–39). It was an image drawn from Ezekiel's vision, in which waters were seen flowing out from God's temple, making the desert wastes into a garden (*see* 47:1ff). Jesus was promising that in the Holy Spirit, he would reach out through his followers to refresh others and give them *life*. What a gift that is, to be his channels to a thirsty world!

We're only beginning. If God's first and greatest commandment is that we are to love him with all our being, then the power to do that must be the greatest of gifts. If we can begin to learn what it is to love him unreservedly, in response to his love for us, we'll be on the road to real life.

And what about loving other people as the Lord has loved us? That's Jesus' "new commandment." That's Paul's "more excellent way." That's what all of us are called to make "our aim." What could be a better gift than the power, deeply and truly, to love?

We're thinking in this whole book about prayer—prayer as calling and as gift. I strongly want to be able to pray better, don't you? To have a praying spirit, a disposition to turn toward God, a heart to call on him in all of life, seems to me a very great gift.

My lifework has been the preaching of the gospel. I have tried to do that as a pastor, as an evangelist, as a teacher of preachers. Now I am privileged also to proclaim the Word by radio and through the printed page. Nothing seems more important to me than doing that well. Every day I find rising within me afresh a longing to be able to preach the Word clearly, faithfully, boldly, in the Spirit's power

Often I dwell on these familiar words of the prophet Micah:

> ...what does the LORD require of you,
> but to do justice, and to love kindness,
> and to walk humbly with your God? (6:8).

That's something to ask for, isn't it, to act with justice, to prize compassion, and to go along step-by-step in communion with God—penitently, trustingly, gratefully? That's what he requires; it is surely also among the "good things" he offers.

The high priestly prayer of Jesus sums up best for me what seems "good." The disciples overheard him saying this to his Father: "'I have glorified thee on earth, having accomplished the work which thou gavest me to do...'" (John 17:4). That was the story of his life. That's what I, in my wiser moments, see as supremely worthwhile. If that could be said of us at the close of life, with any truth, in any measure, we would be blessed indeed. And if that, friends, is a marvelous boon, shall we not ask for it as long as we live?

"But," someone objects, "there's more to all that than just asking for it." Certainly. We need, as we often say, to give "feet to our prayers." We need to put our prayers to work—without a doubt. But how can that be a reason for not asking—an objection to prayer—especially when God has invited us to ask?

Many years ago I was moved and encouraged by a question from John Wesley. He was commenting on a verse from the Epistle of James, "You do not have because you do not ask" (4:2). "How humble," wrote

Wesley, "how joyful, how full of love to God and man we might have been, had we only asked?"

I surely don't mean to say that these I've mentioned are the only "good gifts." Your list may be different and better. Nor am I implying that "character" gifts or "ministry" gifts are the only important ones. Our Lord has taught us to pray for blessings as mundane and common as our daily bread, for healing, for help in a host of practical needs.

In fact, Paul urged his Christian friends in Philippi not to be anxious, but "...in everything by prayer and supplication with thanksgiving let your requests be known to God" (Phil. 4:6). Nothing, apparently, is out-of-bounds, for a believer's petitions. Anything that concerns us, that threatens to make us anxious, anything our hearts cry out for, is to be offered to God as a request, as a supplication freighted with thankfulness.

But why, someone wonders, does God want us to do all this asking? If he knows our need, why must we ask? If he is infinitely good and knows us better than we know ourselves, what point is there in our petitions? Could it be that God sees prayer itself as the very thing we need most? What if asking opens the way for him to meet our greatest need—our need of him? What if this were his way, his all-wise appointed way, of giving himself to people? Friends, believe it. That's what prayer is.

God wants to give himself to us, to bring us, as George MacDonald once put it, "to his knee." He could provide us with all that we want, of course, without our asking. But our having these various needs met is not his chief end in inviting us to pray. You might even say that God withholds so that we may ask. Our need prompts the asking, which leads in turn to communion with him. That is the great goal of prayer, and of everything else.

Here's a child who has run away. Willful and stubborn, he won't return. But in time, hunger drives him back home. He may or may not be fed immediately when he arrives, but he really needs his mother more than his dinner. He may not know that. He might never discover or appreciate it without the hunger pangs that bring him back to her.

For us, too, the need to be with God is the greatest of all our needs. Prayer—the prayer of asking, whatever the felt need that moves us—has a way of doing that. It brings us near God.

We were thinking earlier about good gifts. Anyone knows that the best of gifts is one in which the giver is truly present and imparts himself. This is always the case with God's gifts. His promise is sure: to those who ask and seek and knock, he gives the Holy Spirit. Whatever we ask in faith, trusting in his steadfast love, God answers by giving himself. In the blessing of the Spirit, God's gracious, life-giving presence, God gives us—along with every answer to prayer—the very best!

For Response and Resolve

Since God has invited me to ask, seek, and knock, and since he will not withhold from me any needed blessing, let me ask each day for his good gifts.

For Reading and Meditation

Luke 22:31, 32
Ephesians 1:15–23; 3:14–19; 6:18–20
1 Timothy 2:1–8
Hebrews 7:23–25

For Reflection and Discussion

1. Evaluate the idea that asking for God's gifts is an inferior, immature form of prayer.

2. In what sense does God sometimes say *no* to say a greater *yes*?
3. Why, do you suppose, is it important to him that we should *ask*?
4. What are the "good gifts" which you most desire from God? Are you asking for them?

10

The Call to Intercession
Pleading for Others

"Simon, Simon, behold, Satan demanded to have you, that he might sift you like wheat, but I have prayed for you that your faith may not fail; and when you have turned again, strengthen your brethren" (Luke 22:31, 32).

First of all, then, I urge that supplications, prayers, intercessions, and thanksgivings be made for all men, for kings and all who are in high positions, that we may lead a quiet and peaceable life, godly and respectful in every way (1 Tim. 2:1, 2).

Intercession [is] a complete turning. . . to God, a becoming one with the will of God to the point of self-sacrifice.

Walter Eichrodt

Y ou are invited to pray for others. That could be the greatest good you will ever do them. It could be your best kindness, your most significant service.

Think how important intercession was to Jesus. We don't know all that he prayed about in his early morning times of communion with the Father, in night vigils, and in various retreats to the wilderness. But his disciples were given hints that a great part of his prayer ministry was focused on them. Remember how he said to Peter once, "...I have prayed for you, that your faith may not fail" (Luke 22:32)? Can we doubt that he prayed in that way for the other disciples, too? Surely the long night of sustained prayer before he chose the twelve included earnest petitions for each of them (Luke 6:12).

But his prayer for others went beyond that inner circle. On the night before he was crucified, the disciples overheard him praying, "I do not pray for these only, but for those who believe in me through their word..." (John 17:20). Every person who will ever confess Jesus as Lord was included there. Nor was his concern limited to those who loved and trusted him. Hear his pleading from the cross for his mockers and murderers: "Father, forgive them, for they know not what they do..." (Luke 23:34).

Not only did he pray for others throughout his earthly ministry and with his dying breath—he also continues that praying now as the risen, exalted Lord. According to the witness of the writer to the Hebrews, Jesus "always lives to make intercession" (7:25) for his people. His incarnation and obedience, his suffering and death, his resurrection and ascension—all led up to this: Jesus is "at the right hand of God...interceding for us" (Rom. 8:34). To pray for others is his crowning, continuing ministry. Think of that—the risen One forever lives to plead for you and me, to represent us before God's throne!

That is the calling we are invited to share. We who believe in Christ are welcomed as intercessors along with him, as his partners in prayer for others. For us, too, it is to be a continuing enterprise, a lifelong ministry.

The apostle Paul, for one, had caught the vision of that. He told his fellow Christians that he prayed for them "night and day ...without ceasing," he wrote, "I mention you always in my prayers" (Rom. 1:9). Busy pastor and church planter though he was, Paul could not imagine living for a single day without prayer for others.

What did the apostle ask when he remembered others before God? His letters give us welcome light on that. As far as his unbelieving countrymen were concerned, he wrote, "my heart's desire and prayer to God for them is that they may be saved" (10:1). He counseled prayer "for kings and all who are in high positions, that we may lead a quiet and peaceable life, godly and respectful in every way" (1 Tim. 2:2). When would-be friends deserted him, Paul prayed that their unfaithfulness might not be charged against them (2 Tim. 4:16).

We know most about his prayers for fellow believers. He often disclosed what his petitions for them included. Surprisingly to us, these were not crisis-oriented. His intercessions were not always directed toward the specific problems and troubles of the faithful. He seemed to pray a great deal for Christians who, as far as we can see, were getting along well. In some cases, he prayed for them precisely because he had heard of their "faith in the Lord Jesus" and their "love to all the saints" (Eph. 1:15). What could he ask for such notable, active believers?

In brief, he wanted them to know God. "I do not cease to give thanks for you," he wrote to the Ephesians, "remembering you in my prayers, that the God of our Lord Jesus Christ, the Father of glory, may give you a spirit of wisdom and revelation in the knowledge of him" (vv. 16, 17). They already "knew" God, of course. They had learned to call him "Father" through Christ. But Paul was aware that in knowing the Almighty there is always *so much more!*

He prays later in this Ephesian letter that his Christian friends "may have power to comprehend with all the saints what is the breadth and length and height and depth, and to know the love of Christ which surpasses knowledge..." (3:18, 19). That's the same idea. He wants believers to know how vast are the dimensions of Christ's love, and how our best knowledge of him is like a kindergartner's first lesson.

The "riches" of Christ, according to the apostle, are "unsearchable" (v. 8). They are like a territory we can never fully explore—like depths we can never sound. We grow to know him increasingly, but there is always more to apprehend. We walk around the curving edge of what appears at first to be a lovely lake, only to discover that it is one small inlet of the boundless ocean.

Paul prays that his friends may be given inner strength, divine fullness, spiritual vision, knowledge of God's will. He wants them to lead a life worthy of the Lord, fully pleasing to him, bearing fruit in every good work. He longs to see them able to endure the worst with joyfulness, always giving thanks to God. And all of this, he envisions, will come to them as they are "increasing in the knowledge of God" (Col. 1:10). This was the heart of his intercession: that people everywhere would know the living Lord.

Let that be our focus, too. Let's pray indeed for the current needs of those we love. Let's bear up before the throne the troubles and sorrows of stricken people everywhere. But let's never forget to ask for each the very best: that the God of all grace may make himself increasingly real to them, that they may know him.

Does it make a difference, this intercession for others? Christians surely believe that Jesus' prayers were effectual. He said to Peter, "I have prayed for you, that your faith may not fail" (Luke 22:32). Wasn't he expressing by that a deep assurance? Wasn't he saying that those very prayers would keep Peter's faith alive in the darkest of times? Yes, and doesn't his continuing intercession prevail for us? Listen to the witness of Hebrews: "He is able for all time to save those who draw near to God through him, since he always lives to make intercession for them" (Heb. 7:25). How full of power are the Savior's prayers!

But what about ours? Do they accomplish anything? Dare to believe that they do. Because we are "in Christ," joined by the Spirit to the risen Jesus, our prayers are linked with his. Not only from the right hand of the Father, but from within our hearts, he pleads for his people. As the Spirit moves us to intercede for others, we are sharing in the Lord's own prayers before the throne.

Could those supplications, born in heaven and breathed on earth, prayed by us and presented by him, possibly be in vain? No. To lift our hearts in believing prayer for others may be the most profoundly productive thing we ever do. It links us with the loving, saving purpose of the Almighty. It channels his all-sufficiency to the world's aching need.

"But wait a minute!" the objection comes. "If God wants it, if Jesus is praying for it, won't it happen anyway, whether or not I 'join in'? How can you say that the prayers of this or that believer have any effect? They don't change God's mind, certainly. How can they bring about anything new?"

We all tend to think in that way, don't we? Our structures of logic, valuable and useful as they are, sometimes have a way of imprisoning us. If God is in sovereign control of the universe, we reason, how can our decisions and actions make any real difference? Or, if what we do somehow shapes the scheme of things, how can he be "running the show"?

Strangely, the biblical writers seem untroubled by such neatly packaged systems. Having been encountered by the living God, and having responded to his call, they view human history as marvelously open. They believe in God's sovereign freedom, *and* in the freedom of his people. They know that he is Lord of all, and that we are at the same time responsible agents. They have glimpsed this awesome reality: the God who acts has provided for the significant action of his people. He has made room for them. By their choices and actions, their plans and prayers, they make a difference. Count on it. However the systems of shortsighted reason may seem to deny it, our loving intercessions still bless the world.

George MacDonald, the mentor of C.S. Lewis, once put it this way: "And why should the good of anyone depend on the prayer of another? I can only answer with the return question, 'Why should my love be powerless to help another?'" God in his grace has been pleased to give our love power and to make our prayers fruitful. Hallelujah!

What a beautiful expression of love it is, then, when others pray for us! They are giving us an incomparable gift. A student in one of my seminary courses on prayer once came to me after class to talk about a couple who had befriended him. They knew in his high school days that he was planning to become a minister, and had begun to pray for him regularly. All through high school, all through college years, and now during his seminary training, they had prayed every day for him and his future ministry. As he told me about that, his eyes suddenly filled with tears. He wept unashamedly. It seemed overwhelming to him that this family had cared for him like that. He felt deeply *loved.*

I remember that conversation so vividly because it awakened similar feelings in me. I have a friend named Steve who has battled for almost thirty years with multiple sclerosis. For long periods during that time he has suffered almost constant pain, pain which specialists were unable either to explain or relieve. Steve has spent literally hundreds of nights awake because sleep proved impossible. The pain was too piercing, too relentless.

But marvelous to tell, Steve hasn't lost his sanity. He hasn't become a bitter, complaining man. Through all of his ordeal, he has kept on caring for other people; my family and I are among those for whom he prays. Not a day passes, and scarcely a night, when Steve is not interceding for those he loves. He assures me every time I talk to him that he is still praying for me.

How can I describe what that means to me? Simply to be thought of, to be remembered by others, is no small comfort. To know that we are prayed for even occasionally can warm the heart. But to be the focus of someone's intercession night and day, to be enriched again and again through a friend's woundedness, is so moving as to leave us wordless. It's humbling, almost frightening. I feel profoundly indebted to Steve. I feel touched through him by a grace I can't begin to deserve or repay. And when I face the possibility that he may not live much longer, it seems to me that I am about to lose one of my chief supports in life: brother in Christ, loyal friend, faithful intercessor.

Like all who genuinely pray for others, Steve has always been ready to do more than pray. His prayers are the expressions of a caring that would go to any length. He and his lovely wife, Charlotte, were always there for us when we needed them. If we were at our wit's end in trying to care for a brain-injured son, they would offer to take Billy home with them for a few hours. When Billy needed to be in a special school, they organized financial help for that, providing a great deal of it themselves— behind the scenes. In the days when Steve was strong and active, he would often stop by my study early in the morning to encourage me and pray with me. He taught me what intercession means—and costs.

Often we don't see as clearly as Steve does the commitment involved in praying for others. In the thought world of the Bible, intercession is serious business. When you do it, you put your life on the line for someone else.

Moses, for example, was one of storied intercessors of Old Testament times. He prayed much for the wayward flock he had been called to lead. When the Israelites forsook the Lord to worship gods of their own making, he was furious. But when a well-deserved judgment was about to descend on them, this was Moses' prayer: "Alas, this people have sinned a great sin. They have made for themselves gods of gold. But now, if thou wilt forgive their sin—and if not, blot me, I pray thee, out of the book which thou hast written..." (Exod. 32:31). He was identified with his people, for good or ill, all the way.

God had threatened to consume the rebels and begin again with Moses, his faithful servant. "Of *you*," came the divine promise, "I will make a great nation" (v. 10, italics added). But Moses declined the honor. In spite of all their wandering and ingratitude, the twelve tribes were still his people. He asked in his prayer that they might be forgiven, but if that could not be, Moses was ready to perish with them. He was an intercessor.

At an even deeper level, our Lord identified himself totally with those for whom he prayed. In asking that his people might be saved and his enemies forgiven, he offered himself on behalf of all. It was as though he said, "I'm praying for these, Father. I give myself to you for them, to do or suffer whatever is needful." Prayer was for him the costliest of commitments. Those he prayed for, he was willing to die for.

Have you ever thought about intercession in that way? Without a willingness to be vulnerable for others, what can it mean for us to pray for them? Every genuine prayer for another person includes both a vow and a risk. The vow implied is that we ourselves will do anything in our power to see that prayer answered, that need met. The risk is that sacrifice and suffering may be called for on our part.

Let's dwell on that for a moment. Can we pray earnestly for hungry people without being willing to share our bread with them? Can we plead sincerely with God for a man's conversion to Christ without a readiness to share the Good News with him, to do what we can to give him a chance to hear? Can we pray real prayers for our children to grow up in the faith if we make no effort to live faithfully before them and to teach them of Christ? When we truly pray for others, suddenly our lives are engaged, aren't they? Our comfort and security are at risk. Haven't we said in those prayers for others, "We want the best for them, Lord, at any cost to us"?

But don't let that scare you off. You don't need to wait until you're totally committed to people before you can begin praying for them. You only need a spark of the Lord's love to get started. The very act of praying for others can kindle the spark into flame.

Some of the most interesting research in psychology these days is demonstrating remarkably how feelings follow action. Attitudes are shaped by behavior. If it is true that we act lovingly toward people because we care for them, it is also true that we grow to love them more as we act toward them in caring ways.

You know how that works in your prayers. Suppose there is someone whom you have a difficult time liking. Though you have little heart for it at first, you begin to pray for that person. You keep it up. As time goes on, your feelings change. You begin to see that hard-to-like someone through new eyes. Now it becomes difficult *not* to like her or him! Your intercessions change you. People mean more to you after you have prayed for them.

And that's not all. Praying for others actually prompts you to act on their behalf. Prayer calls them to mind, starts you thinking about them, makes you freshly sensitive to their needs and concerns. Sometimes my intercessions have led me quite directly to write a letter, place a phone call, plan a visit, make an apology, or send a gift. The more we intercede for people, the more likely we are to reach out to them in other ways. It's marvelous how that works!

Should you use a "prayer list" to help you remember persons you want to pray for? That can certainly help. If God should awaken in you a concern to pray for another person, that's too important to leave entirely to your unaided memory. When I write down the names of persons like that, and review the list later, it's often an "Aha!" experience for me. I say to myself, *Oh, yes! How could I have forgotten?* The list helps me to follow through. It stirs me to intercessions that I would otherwise have neglected.

But I also grow weary at times of my prayer lists. For one thing, they tend to get longer and longer! I look at those imposing columns of names and suddenly I'm weary. It begins to seem a mountainous task to pray for them all. I can find myself zipping through the list, almost without thought or feeling. Something about that doesn't seem right. It feels mechanical, contrived. So sometimes I put away the list for a while and run free. But then when I begin to forget loved names, I feel the need of a list again. So it goes.

Maybe you're like I am. You need both discipline *and* freedom, both structure *and* spontaneity. You're always moving somewhere between those two poles. My advice: in all your intercessions, begin by asking the Holy Spirit to direct you. Use a prayer list when it helps you, but feel free to set it aside when it doesn't. As you keep open to people, your working "list" will probably keep changing.

I hope you will view this calling seriously enough to set aside definite time for it. In the midst of John Wesley's amazingly full days, he reserved a late afternoon half-hour specifically for intercession. Others do that in the early morning or at an open time slot during the day. Still others intercede best at day's end, before they retire for the night.

But earnest prayer for others can go on anytime, anywhere. You can send up swift arrows of concern amid the common round of every day's activity: for persons you meet on the street, for those you talk to on the telephone, for those who ask you a question or offer you service. Every encounter with someone's need or pain can find you lifting your heart to God in caring supplication. Intercession can become a way of living with people, a hidden way of loving them.

Sometimes it may not even involve mentioning their names or rehearsing their needs before God. We may simply look on them, or call their faces to mind as we commend them to him.

Charles Whiston, who has written one of the finest of contemporary books on prayer, carries about with him this vivid image of what it is to intercede:

> We may imagine the great towering Jesus Christ, transcending our little world, looking at our world and at us. We come to him. We stand at his feet so small before him, looking up into his face... Then suddenly we realize that he is looking not at us, but beyond and behind us. We feel the strong pressure of his hands on our shoulders, making us turn. We look with him at the world, and as we do so, we find ourselves seeing much more deeply and penetratingly. Without any effort on our part, we receive into our lives his kind of caring for the world. And above and behind us, we hear him interceding for the world to the Father. As we look at the world he loves, and especially those around us, our interceding becomes the echo of his prayer.

Isn't that a rich image? We look at people through the Lord's eyes, and enter for them into his prayers. Sharing his vision, we begin to pray—sometimes wordlessly— with traces of his compassion.

The more we learn of Christ, and the more our own lives are touched by sorrow, the more sensitive we become to the suffering of others. We see its myriad forms, we watch what it does to people, we sense something of their anguish. The sheer mass of suffering—and the awful intensity of it—weigh us down. Where can we go with it except to God?

What do we owe these sufferers? At least our prayers. Shall we not look with Christ for some moment in each

day at the hungry and the homeless, at children neglected and abused, at those stricken with bodily pain or
torment of mind? Shall we not remember, if only briefly,
the oppressed and imprisoned, the addicted ones, the
victims of crime and brutality? Can we forget entirely the
lonely, the despairing, the lost? "Oh, God," we cry, "look
in mercy upon these, relieve their distress. Show us how,
in our small circles, we are to care for and serve them. Be
with them in their night of weeping, and let joy be theirs
in the morning!"

Now for a final invitation to this interceding life. Imagine one of those needy ones right now appealing to you in
Alfred Lord Tennyson's words:

> More things are wrought by prayer
> Than this world dreams of. Wherefore, let thy voice
> Rise like a fountain for me night and day.
> For what are men better than sheep or goats
> That nourish a blind life within the brain,
> If, knowing God, they lift not hands in prayer
> Both for themselves and for those who call them friends?
>   *(Morte d'Arthur)*.

You are invited to answer that call, and to become for
many that kind of friend.

For Response and Resolve

Constrained by his love, let me daily bear up the needs of
others before his throne.

For Reading and Meditation

Matthew 7:7–11
Luke 11:9–13
Philippians 4:6, 7
James 1:5–8; 4:1, 2

For Reflection and Discussion

1. What do you know about the intercessory prayers of Jesus?
2. What did Paul chiefly ask for on behalf of his fellow Christians? What significance do you see in this?
3. On what basis do you believe (if you do) that our prayers for others "make a difference"?
4. In what sense does intercessory prayer involve both a vow and a risk?
5. Discuss the pros and cons of "prayer lists."
6. Which part of your day can you best use for intercession?

11

The Call to Kingdom Concern
Praying for God

And at the time of the offering of the oblation, Elijah the prophet came near and said, "O LORD, God of Abraham, Isaac, and Israel, let it be known this day that thou art God in Israel, and that I am thy servant, and that I have done all these things at thy word. Answer me, O LORD, answer me, that this people may know that thou, O LORD, art God, and that thou hast turned their hearts back (1 Kings 18:36, 37)."

Father, glorify thy name... (John 12:28a).

Prayer should rise more out of God's Word and concern for his Kingdom than even out of our personal needs, trials or desires.

P.T. Forsyth

You are invited to pray for God. How does that strike you? It jarred me when I first tried to put the thought into words. I had never heard anyone express it in that way. But it's exactly what I mean to say. Christians have a life-long calling to pray for God.

I know that sounds strange. I can almost hear someone protest, laughingly: "What do you mean, 'pray for God'?" Isn't he rather the One to whom prayer is offered,

125

and the One who answers it? Besides, what need could
the Almighty have of our small prayers?

I hear that. The thought seems strange to me, too.
I have as much trouble as anyone else taking in the
wonder of it. But I have no doubt at all that we are meant
to pray for God. Jesus expressly told us to do so.

Think about how the Lord's Prayer begins. After addressing God as "our Father," we are to say: "Hallowed
be thy name; thy kingdom come; thy will be done."
Those are not statements, but petitions—not affirma-
tions merely—but prayers. We are, literally, to ask of
God: "Let your name be regarded as holy; let your kingdom come; let your will be done on earth as it is in
heaven." In those prayers we beseech God to do something—on his own behalf. We pray that he will cause his
name to be revered, his reign to be realized, his purpose
to be accomplished. We want that. We plead for it. We
are concerned for him and his cause on earth. We pray
for God.

Further, Jesus teaches here that such praying for God
is to take priority over everything else we pray. We are
invited freely in the Lord's Prayer to ask for our needs
and those of others: daily bread, forgiveness, deliverance
from every evil power. But those are to be the petitions of
people whose first concern is for God—for his name, his
kingdom and his will.

Why is that? Why do you suppose God wants us to
pray in that way? Consider this as an answer: life follows
prayer. As we pray, so we live.

There is a sense in which every human being prays
—all the time. From every heart goes up some great,
sustained longing. We are quivering bundles of desire, all
of us. Some know the One to whom they are crying out;
others do not. But what we are all praying for, at the
deepest level of life, is simply what we want most. What is
the *summum bonum* for you—the highest good? What

do you long for most eagerly, prize above all? What for you seems to offer the height of happiness, the greatest fulfillment? That is your life prayer, and what that prayer is seeking can rightly be called your "god."

How would I know if money, and all it represents, is my idol, my chosen deity? Or how could I tell if power over others had become that to me, or if the love of pleasure had captured my heart, or the passion to make a name for myself? I could begin by examining my behavior—how I use my time, how I invest my resources, how I make my decisions. That would give me significant clues, but it might not be conclusive.

My deepest, steadiest desires can tell best. If I could face honestly my strongest yearning, my ruling passion, I would know whose worshiper I am. What do my thoughts spring back to when they are suddenly disengaged from pressing concerns? Which interest keeps reviving in me, while others come and go—flame up only to fade? What is the treasure for which I would finally trade —everything? That's it. That's my life prayer. That's the something or someone I really call "Lord."

When we become Christians, we don't begin for the first time to pray. We've been doing something like that all our lives, even though we may never have called it "prayer." We've been making some kind of appeal to the future, some draft on the unseen. What happens is that in conversion our prayers are converted. Our life direction is changed. We are praying now in a new way, to a new Lord.

When Jesus taught his disciples the Lord's Prayer, he was responding to a specific request. "Lord, teach us to pray," they asked, "as John taught his disciples" (Luke 1:1). In other words, they wanted to learn to pray *as Jesus' followers*. They asked for a way of praying especially appropriate for those who belonged to him.

That is exactly what he gave them. The Lord's Prayer is Jesus' gift to his people. It is for those who have learned

through him to call God "Father." It is for those who have
abandoned themselves to him, who share his life and
receive his Spirit. They are the ones for whom he will die,
whom he will redeem and transform. In this prayer he
tells them both what their life prayer ought to be and
what it can become. What he commands, he gives—a
new prayer, a new heart.

How did Jesus mean for us to use the Lord's Prayer?
He clearly intended for it to be prayed *frequently,* even
daily. Why else the words "Give us this day our daily
bread"? He surely had in mind also that we should pray it
corporately. The One to whom we appeal is *our* Father;
the food we seek, the forgiveness and deliverance, are for
us. And the church has always believed that the prayer
was to be prayed as nearly as possible "word for
word"—just as Jesus spoke it.

But I'm convinced he had other intentions also. As we
noted earlier, he was teaching us by the order of the
petitions to "put first things first," to "get our priorities
straight." And he was giving us also a guide, an outline, a
framework for all our praying.

Surely Jesus wanted his followers to ponder what
these basic petitions involve. What does it mean for
God's name to be hallowed? What are we seeking when
we ask for that? How could we recognize God's answer
when it came?

I ask myself questions like that frequently. How is God
glorified in this world? How does his name come to be
revered, regarded as holy? Certainly it must first be
known. Before anyone can honor God's name, he or she
must learn it. When we ask, "Hallowed be your name,"
therefore, we are praying that people everywhere may
realize who God is, that they may trust in him, worship
him and honor him.

God's name, remember, is his self-disclosure, his revealed character. We learn his name when he speaks to

us, when he tells us about himself. In turn, we make his name known when we proclaim his Word to others. The grand first petition, then, is a prayer for the worldwide preaching of the gospel.

When I try to explore what this means for my praying, I'm led to pray for all those throughout the world whom God has raised up to proclaim his Word. I ask that each be sustained, empowered, and made fruitful. I pray for all who are preparing for such ministry in Bible schools, colleges, and seminaries, that they may be grounded in the Word, filled with the Spirit, guided and kept. And I ask that wherever in the world the harvest is still great but the laborers few, that God will, according to his promise, thrust out many more laborers. I look toward and pray for that coming day when the "earth will be filled with the knowledge of the glory of the LORD, as the waters cover the sea" (Hab. 2:14). Then, it seems to me, the prayer will be fully answered; God's name will be finally hallowed.

The prayer involves more than evangelism. God's name is hallowed when his people show forth his likeness. When they are faithful and obedient, his holy name is "sanctified" among them. A watching world sees their good works and is led to glorify him. When, on the other hand, they sin against him, they bring disgrace on his name. His name is profaned through them. When they profess to know him, but in behavior deny him, his name is blasphemed and ridiculed.

Once a young member of the church I served was arrested for a sordid crime. When he was taken into custody on a Sunday morning, he happened to be carrying a large Bible. That picture of him appeared the next day in all the newspapers. As some of our members arrived at work in a local factory, they were greeted with this derisive question: "What do you think of your Jesus now?"

When we pray, "Let your name be hallowed," we are surely asking that God's people be revived and purified. We want him to pour out his Spirit on his church, in every communion and congregation. We beseech him to lead his followers to repentance, to transform their lives, to make them a praise to him in the earth.

If the prayer is to be authentic (and more than a bland generality), we are asking these things for ourselves as well as for others. "Lord, send forth your Word," yes, "and use me as you will to make your name known." "Lord, purify your people, and let my life show forth your praise." All this we are seeking and expecting in the first and greatest of our prayers for God: "Hallowed be thy name."

How does his "kingdom come"? He is already "King of kings" and "Lord of lords." What does it mean to ask that his reign should "arrive"? What do we envision as we pray that second petition?

God's "kingdom," in the biblical sense, means the inbreaking of his rule into the midst of our history. The kingdom is not static, but dynamic. It means God's active reign in human lives. To pray for his kingdom to come is to ask that people everywhere may repent, believe the gospel, and submit to the lordship of Jesus. That's what it means to pray that others may become Christians, may be "converted."

We desire also that those who are already his followers may more and more seek his kingdom "first." We long for the time when Christ shall return, when all opposition to his rule shall be ended, when he shall reign forever and ever. We want him to be Lord of our hearts, our homes our societies, our nations. Even as we submit to him now, we pray, "Come, Lord Jesus. Let your kingdom of justice and truth, of peace and love, everywhere prevail."

Much like that is the companion prayer "Thy will be done." Here we are asking that God may be obeyed as fully among us on earth as he is among the angelic hosts about his throne. How do we envision that coming about?

For me it has to do in part with entire nations and cultures. I find myself asking for God's will to be done in the lives of political leaders.

> Father, I pray for those who are in authority over the nations, all kings, presidents, and prime ministers, all governors, legislators, and judges. Turn their hearts toward you. Incline them to rule justly and in your fear. Let them be the servants of your purpose.

I think also of the significant role of the church in God's plan. Is not our obedience as the Lord's people a vital part of his strategy? I want to pray for the worldwide church, that those in all the communions and congregations may fulfill his purpose for them.

> Father, let your will be done
>> in our faith and confession. Let that be molded by your Word and Spirit—
>> in our worship of you. Let it be in spirit and in truth—
>> in our ministry to one another within the body, let us build one another up—
>> in our service to human need in the world, make us courageous and compassionate—
>> in our proclamation to all peoples, let us fulfill, Lord, your Great Commission.

Then I think of the particular denomination in which I serve, and of the local congregation to which I belong. I think of my colleagues in ministry, my family members, my own lifework. Father, let your will be done in us, through us, with us!

The more we reflect on these God-centered petitions, seeking to grasp their varied applications, the more fitting and urgent it seems to pray them. And as we do, our whole selves are somehow "drawn along." Life follows prayer. As we pray, so we live.

I'm awed by people who pray for God, who care deeply about his name. I marvel at Moses, praying like this:

> O LORD, why does thy wrath burn hot against thy people, whom thou hast brought forth out of the land of Egypt with great power and with a mighty hand? Why should the Egyptians say, "With evil intent did he bring them forth, to slay them in the mountains, and to consume them from the face of the earth"? (Exod. 32:11, 12).

Do you see what Moses is concerned about here? About the people, of course. He doesn't want to see his fellow Israelites perish. But involved with their fate is a concern that goes even deeper with Moses. The worst thing he can imagine is that Israel's destruction would lead a watching world to dishonor God. The Egyptians would slander God's motives. They would fail to see the wonder of his steadfast, redeeming love.

Does that prayer strike you as unusual—even marvelous? We aren't accustomed to such passion for God's reputation, are we? Some view this petition cynically, I suppose, as though Moses were trying to manipulate God by appealing to divine self-interest! I can only say in response that Moses' entire career as a servant of God suggests a different motivation. He cared about God's name. He couldn't bear to see the Lord mocked and maligned.

Joshua, Moses' successor, had the same outlook. When the armies of Israel suffered an unexpected, humiliating defeat at little Ai, Joshua was crushed. Here is what he prayed:

> O LORD, what can I say, now that Israel has turned their backs before their enemies? For the Canaanites and all the inhabitants of the land will hear of it, and will

surround us, and cut off your name from the earth; and
what wilt thou do for thy great name? (Josh. 7:8, 9).

The final question is the telling one. Israel's destruction would be disaster enough, but the certain outcome
would be more tragic still. God's name, bound up with
the fortunes of his people, would be hopelessly compro-
mised. That thought, even more than the prospect of
defeat, broke Joshua's heart. "O Sovereign LORD," he
seems to plead, "don't let your own cause fail!"

I hear that in the prayer of the psalmist:

> Help us, O God of our salvation,
>   for the glory of thy name:
> deliver us, and forgive our sins,
>   for thy name's sake!
> Why should the nations say,
>   "Where is their God?" (Ps. 79:9, 10).

I hear it also in the fervent petitions of a Daniel for
Jerusalem:

> O LORD, hear; O LORD, forgive; O LORD, give heed and act;
> delay not, for thy own sake, O my God, because thy city
> and thy people are called by thy name (Dan. 9:19).

Above all, I hear it in the Savior's prayers:

> Father, glorify your name… (John 12:28).

In him the passion is pure, the motives unmixed. As
the faithful Servant, the true Son, Jesus prays unfailingly for God. And this prayer dominates and determines his entire ministry. As he prays, so he lives—and
so he teaches us!

For Response and Resolve

Because the hallowing of God's name, the coming of his kingdom and the doing of his will are to be my greatest concerns in life, let me pray for them every day.

For Reading and Meditation

Exodus 32:11–14
Joshua 7:6–9
Matthew 6:7–13, 25–33
John 12:27, 28

For Reflection and Discussion

1. What does it mean to "pray for God"?
2. What lessons, do you think, does Jesus want us to learn from the Lord's Prayer?
3. In what sense does everyone pray—all the time?
4. Discuss the idea that "life follows prayer." What, as nearly as you can determine it, is your "life prayer"?

PART 3

NEW POSSIBILITIES

12

You Can Follow Jesus in Prayer

In these days, he went out into the hills to pray...
(Luke 6:12). And he told them a parable...that
they ought always to pray and not to lose heart
(18:1).

Whereas Jesus Christ was constant in
communion with His Father; felt the need of it,
and exulted in the joy of it; walked with God, and
talked to God; consulted Him, and accepted His
guidance;... so many nowadays of those He died
to save feel little or no impulse to all that; and
either never think of practicing it at all, or do so
only in a hurried and perfunctory fashion.

A.J. Gossip

All that God has given us to make prayer possible and power-filled centers in Jesus. In him we learn to call God Father; by his cross we are welcomed into fellowship. We receive the Spirit by his quickening breath. In him all the promises of God find their *yes*. But the incarnation means even more: Jesus, the Word made flesh, models for us what it is to pray.

Have you ever noticed how much the Gospel writers emphasize Jesus' life of prayer? Mark tells how he prayed early in the morning, "a great while before day" (1:35). John describes an afternoon on which Jesus withdrew from his disciples to a mountain retreat for prayer. And

Luke records one of Jesus' prayer vigils that lasted all night! (See 6:12.)

When I first began to notice these accounts in the Gospels, I was astonished. Whoever heard of a man praying for such long periods of time, at all hours of the day and night? Prayer must have been an urgent, primary concern in Jesus' life. No activity for him was more absorbing, more time consuming.

As I studied the Gospel records with this thought in mind, my amazement grew. At every major milestone in his ministry, Jesus was observed to be praying. The first of these was his baptism in the river Jordan. There, as the heavens were opened, when the Holy Spirit was descending dovelike upon him, while a voice came from heaven saying, "This is my beloved Son..." (Matt. 4:17) Jesus was visibly at prayer.

The next strategic point was the calling of his disciples. Just before he made the momentous choice of twelve men to be his trusted followers, he had been praying all through the night!

When I asked myself, "What other events in the life of Jesus were especially significant?" I thought of Peter's great confession of faith in Caesarea Philippi, "You are the Christ, the Son of the living God" (Matt. 16:16). That marked the first time that Jesus' close friends had acknowledged him as Messiah and Lord. It was a heaven-born confession. Jesus said to Peter after it, "...Flesh and blood has not revealed this to you, but my Father who is in heaven" (v. 17). And just before it happened, Jesus had been seen praying (Luke 9:18).

Remember the transfiguration, that dramatic scene on a mountainside, when Jesus' glory was revealed to his disciples in blinding light, and he was seen conversing with the two Old Testament greats, Moses and Elijah? Luke makes a special point of telling us that Jesus had climbed that mountain to pray, and that the miracle took place while he was actually praying (*See* Luke 9:28, 29.) What could all that mean?

What does it mean that his teaching of the Lord's Prayer to his disciples followed immediately after a time when they had watched him praying? What is the significance of those persistent, impassioned pleas in Gethsemane, when his "hour" had come? And what mean those last prayers on Golgotha, "Father, forgive them..." (Luke 23:34). "My God, my God, why hast thou forsaken me..." (Matt. 27:46). "Father, into thy hands I commit my Spirit" (Luke 23:46)? Did anyone ever pray as often, as long, as ardently as he? Did anyone ever give to prayer a more central, dominant, strategic place in his life than Jesus did?

But prayer for him was not reserved for major crises. It was more than an emergency measure. In addition to these specific occasions of prayer, the Gospels give us hints of Jesus' more regular practice. Notice this report: "...great multitudes gathered to hear and to be healed of their infirmities. But he withdrew to the wilderness and prayed" (Luke 5:15, 16). The Greek construction here suggests strongly that this was not an isolated incident. There were many crowds, many wilderness retirements, many seasons of prayer. We are allowed to glimpse in this account a kind of *pattern* to our Lord's ministry, a rhythm of withdrawal and return. Here was Jesus spending himself in ministry to broken people, then going apart to pray, even while some were still standing in line! Then, refreshed, he returned again to the labor—and the people—he loved. Prayer and work, work and prayer—so ran the music of his days. Now toiling amid the crowds, immersed in human need, power going forth from him; now in the quietness of communion with the Father, renewing his strength. Never had a man prayed as this Man did.

Many people find it surprising that he prayed at all. I'm often asked, in classes or conferences on prayer, why

Jesus needed to pray. If he was God in the flesh, the query runs, couldn't he do everything all by himself? It's plain enough that we ordinary mortals need all the help that we can get, but why should the Son of God—the eternal Word made flesh—have to pray, to ask? Doesn't Scripture itself pose the question, "Is anything too hard for the LORD?" (Gen. 18:14). But here is Jesus, who would seem to need it less than any of us, praying more than all!

That inescapable fact has challenged and stretched my thinking about who Jesus is. It's easy for me to come to the New Testament with a preconceived idea of how God might act and speak if he were to become man. But the Gospel records themselves are the only accounts in existence of what actually happened when he did.

It's true that Jesus made astounding claims about himself: "I and the Father are one" (John 10:30). "…He who has seen me has seen the Father…" (14:9). "All authority in heaven and on earth has been given to me" (Matt. 28:18). He could stretch out his arms to the wide world and say, "Come to me, all you who labor and are heavy laden, and I will give you rest" (11:28). But at the same time, he always spoke of himself as totally dependent on his Father. For him, unique Sonship and divine authority never implied acting "on his own." He emphatically denied that he ever did so, or could: "Truly, truly, I say to you, the Son can do nothing of his own accord…" (John 5:19).

Though he knew himself to be Lord of all, he acted always as a devoted Son, whose one aim was to please the Father. And it was in that way, I began to see, that he has revealed to us what it means to be human. Jesus is our Brother, bone of our bone, flesh of our flesh. He has shared fully our human lot. He can sympathize with our infirmities. He has entered into our sorrows. He has taken on himself our limitations, our vulnerability. And before dying on our behalf, he demonstrated what it is to live a genuinely human life. He trusted in God. He did the Father's will. And, at every point along the way, he prayed.

Does that affect you as it does me? Jesus is the one whom I call "Lord." He is the Teacher; I am one of his learners. It is his to lead, mine to follow. The way for my life must be always "in his steps." What authority then must Jesus' praying have for me?

"Perhaps," someone suggests, "we're dealing with a merely cultural matter here. In all this emphasis on prayer, Jesus was evidently a man of his time. He lived in a religious, prescientific age. People were accustomed to much praying in those days." Nothing could be further from the truth. I was struck by these words from a noted student of the first-century world, Joachim Jeremias:

> At no other point does the inner corruption and decay of the Hellenistic world...in New Testament times become so apparent as in the sphere of prayer.... From ancient comedy onwards, parodies of prayer had become a stock convention for comedians.... Foolish, immoral, ridiculous and even obscene prayers are woven into the action of the play and provoke the audience to uproarious laughter.... Thousands of magical papyri with their masses of abstruse names and epithets are moving tokens of how men had become uncertain about the efficacy of prayer.

Jesus' practice of prayer stands in the sharpest contrast to all that.

It was different also from prayer as his countrymen knew it. Pious first-century Jews observed three daily times for prayer: upon arising in the morning, before bedtime, and at the hour of the afternoon sacrifice in the temple. These prayers consisted of a series of benedictions, often accompanied by recitation of the Shema: "Hear, O Israel, the Lord our God is one Lord." But these prayers were usually brief and stylized. Jesus apparently began with this traditional practice (praying morning, afternoon, and evening) but went far beyond it. There is nothing in the religious world of his time that can possibly account for his remarkable practice of prayer. No, this is part of the new reality that broke on the world in his coming.

His first followers, however, learned from Jesus to pray. He was diligent in teaching them about it, instructing them in what to ask for, assuring them that they would be heard, encouraging them to persevere. On this subject, he never wearied of repetition. "Ask, and it will be given you; seek, and you will find; knock, and it will be opened to you" (Luke 11:9). Then, lest the point be missed, he went over the same ground again: "Every one who asks receives; he who seeks finds, to him who knocks it will be opened" (v. 10). "Watch," he said, "and pray...pray at every opportunity...men ought always to pray and not to lose heart." The disciples began to see that he was urging on them precisely what he had lived by. Prayer expressed more than anything else the dependent, devoted, expectant attitude of his entire ministry. He wanted them to pray as he prayed. In this too, he was saying, "Follow me."

And, do you know—they did! When his work was accomplished, when he had given himself to die for our sins and had been raised from the dead, when he had commissioned his disciples, it happened. They began to adopt his ways in prayer. Study the Book of Acts and notice how many times you find these early Christians praying. It began in that upper room, before Pentecost. Jesus had told them to wait in Jerusalem until they should be endued with power from on high. For them that waiting meant one thing: united, continuing prayer. "All these with one accord devoted themselves to prayer, with the women and Mary the mother of Jesus, and with his brothers" (Acts 1:14). As Jesus had prayed before his baptism in the river Jordan, so they prayed before being baptized with the Holy Spirit.

And that was only the beginning. When on Pentecost Day, thousands were converted to faith in Christ, they were all initiated into a praying community. "They devoted themselves to the apostles' teaching and fellowship, to the breaking of bread and the prayers" (2:42). When persecution arose and the infant church was menaced by the ruling powers, believers turned to prayer. And Luke records, "When they had prayed, the place in which they were gathered together was shaken, and they were all filled with the Holy Spirit and spoke the word of God with boldness" (Acts 4:31).

The apostles, when pressured with many worthwhile responsibilities, decided to give themselves to the supreme priorities of preaching and prayer. Prayer was the first sign that Saul the persecutor had become a believer: "...Behold, he is praying" (9:11). When a new movement of ministry to the Gentiles was about to be launched, the apostle Peter was found praying on a housetop. The history-making missionary tours of Barnabas and Paul were conceived in a gathering for prayer at Antioch. These early Christians prayed by the seashore, in upper rooms, from oriental dungeons, and under the worst physical abuse. It was enough for them that they should be as their Master: praying Lord, praying people.

Why, I wondered, had I never seen that before? The New Testament witness was plain enough. It seemed to me that the prodigious prayerfulness of Jesus and his first followers had been a closely guarded secret in the church as I had known it. George Buttrick in *Prayer* had noted the same phenomenon in his generation: "Even the best biographies," he wrote, "fail to do full justice to His practice of the Presence." And somehow the contemporary call to trust in Jesus has rarely included a summons to follow him in prayer.

I think I see some of the reasons for that now. Perhaps the activist strain in American Christianity has something to do with it, our strong emphasis on practical programs, visible results. Perhaps it's our fear of what theologians call "pietism," a sentimental other-worldliness that retreats from engagement with its surrounding culture. But perhaps, more than anything else, our scant attention to prayer betrays our feebleness of faith.

Suppose you wanted, in your life, in your circle, to see all that changed? Suppose you felt deeply that prayer is the open secret of Christian vitality, the "one thing needful" for followers of Jesus? Suppose you wanted to learn from him to pray? What would you do? Where would you start?

If you're like I am, the prospect of praying as Jesus did, or even as his disciples did, is downright intimidating. However needful and desirable it may be, it seems an impossible goal. I know at least a little bit about my own laziness and lack of discipline, my flickering motivation, and wandering thoughts. And I can well remember past resolutions to become more diligent in prayer. Many of them have trickled away like tiny streams of water in the sands of a desert. Is there any real hope for a change?

I write this because I deeply believe there *is* hope. Don't expect to become a prayer athlete, a prayer expert overnight, or in a few weeks, or *ever,* for that matter! We're always learning in this school. Prayerfulness is not like a blob of bubble gum that can be stretched instantly to any desired length. It's more like a muscle that grows stronger with steady, vigorous use. Don't make the mistake of trying to pray all night before you've had some success at praying for ten minutes! But do expect to *grow!* We cannot walk immediately or exactly in the giant steps of our Redeemer, but we can begin to follow him. We can set our hearts to make prayer central in our lives as he did in his.

We can trust that Jesus, the Living Lord, is still teaching his disciples to pray, still empowering them by his Spirit. He, the praying one, abides with us. In spite of all our weakness and faintheartedness we can find courage in him to make headway. We can follow Jesus—in prayer.

For Response and Resolve

Whenever I pray, let me look to Christ as my Lord and Teacher, seeking to model my praying after his.

For Reading and Meditation

Mark 1:35–39
Luke 3:21, 22; 5:15, 16; 6:12–19; 9:18–20, 28, 29
John 11:38–44
Acts 1:12–14; 4:29–31; 6:4; 13:1–3

For Reflection and Discussion

1. What especially impresses you about Jesus' practice of prayer?
2. Why did he, as God's Son, need to pray?
3. How did Jesus' praying differ from that of his contemporaries?
4. Does an awareness of how Jesus prayed seem encouraging or discouraging to you? Explain your answer.

13

You Can Keep It Up

And he said to them, "Which of you who has a friend will go to him at midnight and say to him, 'Friend, lend me three loaves; for a friend of mine has arrived on a journey, and I have nothing to set before him'; and he will answer from within, 'Do not bother me; the door is now shut, and my children are with me in bed; I cannot get up and give you anything'? I tell you, though he will not get up and give him anything because he is his friend, yet because of his importunity he will rise and give him whatever he needs" (Luke 11:5–8).

Pray constantly (1 Thess. 5:17).

To cultivate the ceaseless spirit of prayer, use more frequent acts of prayer. To learn to pray with freedom, force yourself to pray. The great liberty begins in necessity.

P.T. Forsyth

We've been thinking together about prayer as God's gift and our calling. I've said more than once that I think it's meant to be a *lifelong* calling. I hope you share that conviction. Let me underline it now. I believe that in your praying and mine, God prizes *persistence*.

Maybe you're feeling by now that what I've been describing is a lot of work. It tires you to think about it—all that praying! "We're supposed to listen to God in his Word," I hear you say, "to praise and thank him, to confess before him and commit ourselves to him, and that's only the beginning. He wants us also to ask him for good gifts, to intercede for others, to pray for his cause and kingdom on earth. Doesn't that take a lot of time? Who of us, in this busy, hectic modern world, can fit all that into an already crowded schedule?"

Obviously, it does take time—and energy, too. But you can do this at your pace and your discretion. Don't get hung up on the time element. God doesn't count the minutes. It has been liberating for me of late to look on prayer times more in terms of *purpose* than duration. I want each day to pray in these particular ways, with these objectives, but I rarely think about how much time it's taking.

Everything is flexible. The various elements of prayer don't always have to come in the same order, or receive the same emphasis. On some days petition may be paramount for me. At other times I may feel searched in heart, needing very much to confess my wanderings and commit myself afresh. Thanksgiving will often be my major note, or praise. But I find that even in the most hurried stretches of my days there is always opportunity to pursue this life calling, if I am minded to do it.

And let me say another thing about that. Sometimes, when I think about urging on others this commitment of prayer, with all that it involves, I wonder if I'm burdening them down. Am I trying to impose a heavy regimen on people, needlessly complicating their lives? Will they, if they seriously attempt something like this, soon grow weary of it? Will it seem to them dull and distasteful?

At other times, those misgivings simply vanish away, not so much when I try to reason them through, as when I pray. When I do this myself, when I give myself to prayer in these ways, the bedrock assurance comes back: this is important; this is vital; this is what God wants! It seems supremely right to me then to be praising and thanking, confessing, and committing myself, asking for good gifts, pleading for others, praying for God.

I can say more. When I do this, I am, in a way I can't fully describe, refreshed. My zest for living is restored. I get up from praying with new heart for the day. It has for me almost physical effects. I feel better. I feel ready for whatever life has in store. The prophet Isaiah said it: "They who wait for the LORD shall renew their strength..." (Isa. 40:31). I believe that. It happens. After four decades of it, praying is still for me alive and fresh.

I want to be honest about this—duly restrained in what I say. Prayer times don't *always* have this rejuvenating effect on me. Sometimes the going is hard. My mind wanders. The words won't come. A queasy fear comes over me: Am I wasting my time, going through a meaningless routine?

It's rough work for me then to keep going. Sometimes I keep at it anyway. Sometimes I stop, do something different for a while. Sometimes I simply say, "Lord, you know." But I can tell you straight that the times have been very few when some hint of refreshing hasn't eventually come—when God's presence hasn't become newly real to me.

I remember resonating once with a Puritan writer who described his efforts to pray in words like these: "When I begin, my heart is like a huge, heavy stone. But when I struggle with the impossible task of lifting it up to God, I find it gradually becoming lighter. As I continue, it sometimes takes wings and soars like a bird!" I can identify with him. Mercies like that have come to me, too. My heart has been lifted. It's the Spirit's work.

Many writers on the spiritual life describe what is called "the dark night of the soul." They tell how sincere believers, ardent seekers after God, feel sometimes bereft. They go through seasons of "dryness." They lose their taste for holy things. God seems to them infinitely far away. Their spirits languish. They grope in the darkness and see no light.

I think I know what they mean. I have been through such "night" seasons. But all the saints tell us to keep seeking the Lord, anyway, to keep "looking in his direction," even when we catch no glimpse of him. They say that though weeping may endure for a long night, joy will come with the morning. I think they are right, don't you? The light will surely dawn. The seekers at last will find. What strong encouragement to keep on praying!

Have you ever noticed how much Jesus said about persistence in prayer? That was one of his major themes, both in exhortation and parable. Think, for example, about the "friend at midnight" (see Luke 11:5–8).

It was one of the most arresting stories Jesus ever told. Just for a moment, try to "live" yourself into it. You dwell in a small, first-century Galilean village. Just when you're about to retire one night, an old friend appears at the front door. You welcome him warmly and soon discover that he's come a long way. The man is tired and ravenously hungry. It's painfully embarrassing for you, because your cupboard is bare. There isn't even a scrap of bread in the house. What to do? It seems unthinkable to send an honored guest to bed hungry, but it's midnight. No markets are open, and everything is dark.

Then you remember a neighbor down the street who is fairly well-to-do and who always has a supply of food on hand. You hate to bother him, but, well, this is an emergency! So for the sake of your famishing friend, you slip on a coat and venture out into the night. You grope your way from building to building until you brush against the right house. Finding the door at last, you begin to knock. No answer. You knock again, but all is silent within. Almost desperate, you begin to *pound* on the door and call out to your neighbor.

Soon a dog starts barking and is joined by another. A light sleeper down the street wakes with a start and wonders what's going on.

You hear a faint response from within the house. "Who's there?" a voice mumbles. "What do you want?" It's hard to shout through the door, but you tell him who you are and what your situation is. "Friend, lend me three loaves of bread, will you? My friend has come to me from a journey and I have nothing to set before him." "Man," comes the response, "don't bother me at this hour! I've locked up the house; we've just gotten the baby back to sleep. I can't get you any food!"

By now, you're embarrassed, mortified. The whole neighborhood is astir and you're getting nowhere. But you swallow your pride and decide to risk making a nuisance of yourself. You keep on knocking. Finally the man inside can stand it no longer. He gets up, stumbles around in the dark, gathers all the bread he can find, and almost hurls it out the door. "There, take it, and for pity's sake, leave me alone!"

Now after he told that story, Jesus made this comment: "I tell you, though he will not get up and give him anything because he is his friend, yet because of his importunity he will rise and give him whatever he needs" (v. 8). (Note: because of his *importunity*, literally his "shamelessness," his "brazen persistence.") That's what finally got results. And to follow that up, Jesus had this word for his disciples: "Keep on asking and it will be given you. Keep on seeking and you will find. Keep on knocking and the door will be opened to you" (*see* v. 9). In other words, "Be like this undaunted visitor, this importunate friend. When once you go after something, keep plugging away. When once you start to pray, don't give up!"

I've noted for a number of years that some good, thoughtful, religious people have trouble with this idea.

In their view, it seems to run counter to other important teachings of our Lord. Some are uncomfortable with the notion of repeated asking because of an emphasis in the Sermon on the Mount: "And in praying," says Jesus, "do not heap up empty phrases as the Gentiles do; for they think that they will be heard for their many words. Do not be like them, for your Father knows what you need before you ask him" (Matt. 6:7, 8). Doesn't that seem to discourage importunity? Our heavenly Father knows what we need before we ask him the first time. It's wrong to think that our many words will make him hear us. We are not to heap up empty phrases, or as the Authorized Version puts it, "vain repetitions."

But what Jesus is describing here is actually quite different from a man knocking tirelessly to get bread for his friend. Our Lord is forbidding not persistence, but *mindlessness.* He doesn't want us reciting words without thought, prayers without heart. To mumble the same words a hundred times as though they were like the combination that unlocks a safe—that's "heaping up empty phrases." But to ask for something over and over again because our burdened hearts cry out for it—that's *importunity,* that's real prayer.

I've sometimes heard people object to persistent asking on other grounds. They are concerned that prayers should be offered in *faith.* In their view, we need ask God for some gift or blessing only once. Didn't Jesus say, "Whatever you ask in prayer, believe that you receive it, and you will" (Mark 11:24)? So if you ask with a firm trust that the answer is already on the way, what need is there to ask again? Why weary God with further requests when the issue is already settled? Doesn't the fact that we keep on asking betray a lack of faith? It's acting as though we haven't gotten God's attention yet. We're treating him as though he's sleepy or hard of hearing, acting as though his promise to hear us were not true. How much better,

we are told, simply to ask once and then leave it all in
God's hands!

Now that certainly seems plausible, and far less work
than continued praying. But it hardly fits in with the
parable of Jesus about this man who knocked and
knocked and wouldn't stop knocking, or with that similar tale about the widow who kept pestering the unjust
judge (Luke 18:1–8). Finally he took her case, fearing that
otherwise she would wear him out with her endless appeals. Apparently, in Jesus' mind, importunity and faith
are not enemies but friends.

Why, if a loved one is in need or distress, do we keep on
praying for her or him? Is it because we don't believe we
are heard? No, it's because the concern is so constantly
on our minds and because we care so deeply about it. In
prayer to a gracious heavenly Father, we're invited to
pour out our hearts, to make all our wants and wishes
known. And because we keep on wanting his blessing
intensely, we keep on asking for it passionately. The
ceaseless prayer is simply the overflow of a caring heart.

Is there no faith in that? Of course there is! Our unwearied asking may be faith's highest expression! It's
easy to "believe" when we have prayed, and almost before we can snap our fingers, the answer appears. But to
continue praying through long periods when nothing
seems to change, to "hang onto God with our hearts," to
continue beseeching him, to believe as William Cowper
wrote that "behind a frowning providence He hides a
smiling face," that's genuine faith.

Remember the Syro-Phoenician woman who came to
Jesus (Matt. 15:21–28), brokenhearted over her afflicted
daughter? First she cried, "Have mercy on me, O Lord,"
but Jesus said nothing. The disciples seemed more
kindly to her than he. They urged him to do something
for the woman. "Send her away, for she is crying after
us." But he said, "I was sent only to the lost sheep of the

house of Israel." That seemed to rule her out, for she was a Gentile. But she wouldn't quit. She came and knelt before him, saying, "Lord, help me," only to hear Jesus say in response, "It is not fair to take the children's bread and throw it to the dogs."

How would you have felt at that—being referred to as one of the little puppies under the table, with no right to food reserved for the children! But she kept after Jesus. "Yes, Lord," she answered, "yet even the dogs eat the crumbs that fall from their master's table."

How did Jesus react to that persistence? Did he say, "Shame on you for repeating yourself, for asking so much?" Not at all. Did he say, "You should know that one request is sufficient." No. What he said was, "O, woman, great is your faith. Be it done for you as you desire." Whatever Jesus meant by urging people to pray with faith, he never intended to discourage heartfelt, continual pleading. He recognized in a supplication that would not be denied the most beautiful form of believing. That woman of great faith had Jesus smiling with admiration, shaking his head in wonder.

There's one more objection. This one seems weightiest of all. It has to do with submission to God's will. It is sometimes argued that to keep on asking for something is to be unduly assertive, to try to impose our will on God, to bend him, the almighty Lord, to our wishes. Didn't Jesus teach us to be obedient in all things to our heavenly Father? Didn't he himself pray in the Garden of Gethsemane, "Not as I will, but as thou wilt" (Matt. 26:39)?

The answer, of course, is *yes.* But remember that before he prayed that prayer of submission, he asked the Father repeatedly that the bitter cup might be taken away from him. Paul, like his Master, could accept a thorn in the flesh and even glory in his infirmity. But before coming to that point he had asked three times that his painful, humiliating affliction might be taken away.

The point is this: There may come a time when God makes it very plain to us that a cherished desire will not be fulfilled, a sick loved one will not survive, someone we love will choose another, a lingering anguish won't leave us. But until he makes that unmistakably clear, we have the strongest possible encouragement to pray on.

Do our present circumstances always represent God's highest will for us? Hardly. Suppose you were born in abject poverty, into a family where no one had ever received formal education. Does that necessarily mean that it is God's will for you to remain penniless and illiterate? Or are you rather meant to strive against those difficulties, and by God's help to rise above them?

Or suppose you become ill. Is that to be passively accepted as though it were God's design? The whole medical profession exists to say an emphatic "No!" Although it may be our present condition, we ought to resist disease, fully confident that God is on the side of health. If we have a condition that is life threatening, should we begin by accepting death as inevitable? Or should we fight with all our strength for life? There may be a time for acceptance and resignation, but only after we've wrestled, only after we've poured out our hearts in prayer.

We need at times to resist what *seems* to be God's will in favor of the gracious purpose he has made known to us in Christ. Look at Jesus, caring for the scorned, healing the leprous, seeking the unwanted, and dying for the guilty. See him sacrifice himself utterly for our good. That's how God feels about us. He has in mind for us a new creation. Don't submit readily to present miseries and indignities as though they were his high design. Believe him for something better, both for yourself and for those you love, and *ask*. Trust Christ as your Savior. Believe that God is for you and that nothing can ever separate you from his love.

The real question about importunity is this: Does our continued praying actually have an effect on God's will? In one sense, no. God's will is grace. His purpose is salvation for his people. Nothing we do or pray or neglect can change that. But in another important sense, the answer is yes. Our prayer can definitely change his manner of dealing with us.

Let's say that we are living carelessly and God deals with us in a way suited to our condition. But when we become concerned and begin to pray, his manner of working with us alters. Or again we may pray and not be prepared at the time for God's answer. But as we change and grow, as faith becomes deeper and commitment more entire, we become ready for the answer. Then he gives it. Things happen in answer to our prayers that would not otherwise occur. Doors are opened, gifts given, mercies received because we and others have prayed.

Friends, unless we believe that, the life and heart goes right out of our praying. Give up the habit of wrestling and the hope of prevailing, and you have lost the living reality of what it is to pray.

Oh, be sure of this, your prayer can alter God's ways. It can bring mercies from him to you and to others that would not otherwise come. Don't give up. Let nothing discourage you from continued asking. However sensible the objections to it may seem, you have Jesus' authority for this: your importunate prayer is a "wrestling" God loves and to which he often delights to yield.

Never stop seeking God. You may grow weary at times. Discouragement, like a cold mist, may steal over you and chill your spirit. It may seem to you that prayer is enormously difficult, even impossible. You can only groan in helplessness. But even that can be real prayer. Remember that the Holy Spirit, when we don't know how to pray as we ought, makes intercession for us "with sighs too deep for words." He's with us in the groaning, turning it into powerful prayer. The faintest longing to pray is a sign of hope. Cherish that. Don't give up on it.

Sometimes you will stop praying for a time. You'll neglect your "devotions." You'll forget God. You'll be inwardly miserable, but in spite of the emptiness you won't call on him. You'll just muddle along. What then? Is it all over? Does that prove you never really loved him at all, never meant it when you prayed before?

No. You go back to him. You begin afresh. And in returning you realize again how gracious and patient the Lord is. You discover anew that he is the fountain of living waters. You wonder why you ever stayed away, ever stopped calling upon him.

That's how Christians grow. Progress in the life of faith, in the school of prayer, is not an unbroken string of successes. "Ever onward and upward" is not our style. We wander and lose our way. We stumble and fall on our faces. We cop out on our best resolutions. And then, drawn by a love too wonderful to imagine, we somehow get up and head for home again. Once more, we set our vagabond hearts toward God. We pray, and—marvelous to say—he is still there.

Maybe next time we aren't as quick to drift away, and when we do, we're quicker to come back. The lapses aren't as deep as they once were, or as long. Incredibly dense though we are, we're learning. We're learning that his love won't let us go. His Spirit won't abandon us. In spite of our weakness and willfulness, we can fulfill our calling. We can keep on praying.

For Response and Resolve

As God assigns great value to persistence in prayer, let me persevere in spite of delays and disappointments.

For Reading and Meditation

Psalm 116:1, 2
Matthew 15:21–28
Luke 11:5–10; 18:1–8
Ephesians 6:18

For Reflection and Discussion

1. How would you evaluate this statement: "If you ask God for something twice, you must think that he didn't hear you the first time"?
2. Why did Jesus seem to prize "importunity," persistence in asking?

14

You Can Call Others

*O magnify the LORD with me, and let us exalt his
name together! (Ps. 34:3).*

*You also must help us by prayer, so that many
will give thanks on our behalf for the blessing
granted us in answer to many prayers (2 Cor.
1:11).*

It was a lazy summer evening in 1944. I was sitting
under a streetlight near my home in Hastings-on-Hud-
son, New York. My high school friend asked me what I
thought it meant to be a Christian. I didn't have the
haziest idea. After I had stammered and stumbled for a
while, Jack explained the gospel to me. He told me who
Jesus is and what he has done for us all. He showed me
how I could receive the Lord as my Savior and commit
myself to his rule. Jack read the promises of God to me
from the Bible.

All of that was news to me—news amazingly good. It
broke over me like a sunrise. I deeply knew it was true. I
knew that I had gotten in touch with something uniquely
important, with Someone who had claimed me for his
own. I prayed. I thanked my friend. I went home and
woke up my parents to tell them what had happened. If I
had thought of a way to do it, I suppose I would have tried
to tell everyone. The news seemed too urgent, too joyous
to keep to myself.

I later found that sharing the faith is not always easy,
and that some people do not seem eager to listen. My

attempts to communicate the gospel were often clumsy, and I sometimes lacked the courage even to try. But the deep desire to let others know of Christ and his saving love never left me. After all these years, it's still there. If you have embraced the gospel, if you have tasted and seen that the Lord is good, you know what I mean.

I feel that way about prayer, too. Ever since I first called on the Lord, first invited him into my life, prayer has seemed to me the grandest of all privileges. It is incomprehensible to me why everyone would not view it so, if once they knew what it means—if ever they met the Lord. Will the Master of the universe listen to you and me? Will he welcome us into his presence? Will he accept us as beloved children and invite us to call him "Father"? Will we creatures, we sinners, have fellowship with the Holy One? Will he give us everything in giving us himself? Can all this be possible for you and me?

This privilege of prayer, surely, is meant to be shared. We pray individually, often while in solitude, but never alone. We always pray as fellow humans, and as members of a believing community. In prayer we have direct access to God but never a private line. Real prayer is always inclusive, reaching out to others, gathering them in. P.T. Forsyth puts it beautifully:

> Prayer is the great producer of sympathy. Trusting the God of Christ, and transacting with Him, we come into tune with men. Our egoism retires before the coming of God, and into the clearance there comes with our Father our brother (The Soul of Prayer).

The calling to pray, then, is always a call we pass on. We invite others to seek God with us. Taking our cue from the Bible, we make much of *corporate* prayer.

I have known people, some of them genuinely devout, who feel uncomfortable about praying in the presence of

others. They see communion with God as so intensely
personal that they are hesitant to share it. They shrink
from all appearance of self-display. Perhaps they appeal
to Jesus' words in the Sermon on the Mount: "When you
pray, go into your room and shut the door and pray to
your Father, who is in secret; and your Father who sees
in secret will reward you" (Matt. 6:6).

Anyone who has tried to pray aloud in the presence of
others knows something of the danger against which
Jesus warns us. We can become so conscious of the
people around us, so concerned about what they think of
our prayers, that we almost forget we are addressing
God. It is sadly possible to pray for "effect," to convey a
certain image of ourselves to others. We can become like
the "hypocrites" described by Jesus, who "love to stand
and pray standing in the synagogues and at the street
corners, that they may be seen by men..." (v. 5).
Charles H. Spurgeon imagines in one of his sermons how
God must feel about such praying. The Lord is overheard
instructing his angels, "Those prayers were intended for
men; let men have them!"

But surely Jesus never meant by those warnings to
forbid united prayer. He himself prayed in the presence
of his disciples. He taught them a prayer for their common use. In the upper room before Pentecost the believers prayed together, with one accord. In the Book of
Acts alone, I've found at least fifteen recorded instances
of disciples praying in groups. The worship of Christian
congregations ever since has always included some form
of common prayer.

Jesus is speaking in the Sermon on the Mount not so
much about where we pray, or with whom, as about our
motives. He wants us to make sure that we are praying,
not play acting. He's reminding us that whenever we
pray we are to focus on God and not on the impression we
may be making. Even in the midst of a crowd, we are to

be conscious chiefly of the unseen Father. Everything is for his eye, his ear, his heart.

God promises a special hearing to united prayer. James assures us that the fervent prayer of even one righteous person "has great power" (5:16). But God delights to see his people "harmonize" in their requests. Jesus teaches his disciples that if two of them "agree" on earth regarding something they are to ask, it will be done for them by their Father in heaven (Matt. 18:19). Their unity of mind, their concert of will, seems to play a significant part in God's answer.

Remember how James urges Christians "Confess your sins to one another; and pray for one another..." (5:16). He seems to envision a situation of mutual ministry. We hear each other's acknowledgments of sin; we bear each other up before God's throne. The group listens and prays with one accord. And from that openness to each other and to God, comes the gift of healing grace.

> Before our Father's throne
> We pour our ardent prayers;
> Our fears, our hopes, our aims are one,
> Our comforts and our cares.
>
> John Fawcett, 1782

Christians pray together in public worship. Perhaps a number of them pray audibly, perhaps only one. But these are never individual petitions. The prayer of a leader in worship is not "a good man being overheard at his devotions." It is a representative prayer. He or she prays on behalf of the people, as though all appealed to God with one voice. The assembled worshipers participate. Whether by a spoken "Amen" or by inward assent, they make the leader's prayer their own. "Yes, Lord. Let it be so... this we seek... these are our concerns."

But the people of God have never confined their united praying to formal gatherings, stated occasions for worship. In a myriad of smaller configurations, they join their spirits before God; they meet to pray. Sometimes it's the beginning of a joint enterprise or an occasion of parting from loved ones. Sometimes it's around a family meal. Sometimes a crisis summons us to common prayer; sickness, loss, dire calamity. Sometimes our shared joy is so full it keeps overflowing in waves of thanks and praise.

Many of these gatherings for prayer seem spontaneous. They simply happen. Others are planned, and occur with some regularity. But all are initiated by *someone*. Each takes place because a believer, moved by God's Spirit, suggests it. "Let's pray about this... let's bring it to the Lord... let's have a time of thanks." Or maybe it's a question inviting response. "Could we take some time now for prayer?"

I remember how impressed I was a few years ago when I learned how ministry groups are formed at the Church of the Savior in Washington, D.C. As I recall, it goes like this: someone in the congregation becomes aware of a need, or feels a concern to serve in a specific way. The feeling persists; the sense of urgency grows. Then she or he begins to talk with others about that prospect, testing their interest. Perhaps an announcement is made or invitations are given. "I'd like to start a ministry group on behalf of homeless people in our area"; or "I'd like to see if something can be done in this community for latchkey children. How would you feel about being a part of that?"

Someone is issuing a call, offering an invitation: "I'm going to get involved in this. Would you like to join me?" If others sense the concern and express a desire to participate, a group is formed and the new ministry takes shape. And sometimes out of those small, simple beginnings come great things.

Something like that happens whenever people come together for prayer. Someone issues a call; others respond to it. Joined in a common concern, they seek the Lord. They pray together. Who can measure the effects?

Think of the "calls" like that in the Scriptures:

O magnify the LORD with me,
  and let us exalt his name together! (Ps. 34:3).
O come let us worship and bow down,
  let us kneel before the LORD our Maker (Ps. 95:6).
Come, let us return to the LORD....
Let us know, let us press on to know the LORD (Hos. 6:1, 3).

I will always be grateful for those who invited me to pray with them: my first Davidson College roommate, a few fraternity brothers concerned to make Christ known on our campus, a friend who asked me to learn with him the riches of the Greek New Testament. They ministered to me, and our uniting praying seemed to lead again and again to new insight and enlarged witness.

I think of those seminary classmates who welcomed me to pray with them for the work of Christ in Japan. That sparked for me a lifelong interest in that country. Largely through these prayer meetings, Helen and I were led to prepare for missionary service in Japan. We would probably be there now, had it not been for our oldest son's crippling illness. Some of those prayer partners with whom I used to meet are still laboring for Christ in Japan.

I began to learn how strategic such groups can be. In the first congregation we served at Lodi, New Jersey, I invited young people to form a prayer fellowship before school, and groups of adults to pray for "laborers for the harvest." Helen did something like that among the women of the congregation.

We were thrilled and awed at what began to happen. From that small congregation God began to raise up people, one after another, to serve Christ. Three young men and another in middle age went away to college and seminary, preparing for the ordained ministry. Leaders sprang up within the congregation for a variety of new youth programs. A prominent lawyer in our congregation was given a vision for helping juvenile delinquents. All of this seemed to grow out of little bands of Christians, calling on God together.

We saw similar things happen through small prayer groups in a large congregation on the south side of Chicago. One group met on Saturday mornings to pray for inactive members and those who had never professed Christ. We each had a printed list of their names, and were moved to see how one after another was crossed off the list as people came to Christ, or were restored to active membership. One group of young adults met early on weekday mornings to study an ancient creed and to pray for a new outpouring of the Spirit. These men, twenty-five years later, are all devoted servants of Christ, some with key posts of leadership.

I was privileged to teach preaching for ten years at Western Theological Seminary of the Reformed Church in America. There, too, groups for united prayer were centers of Christian vitality. Some were prompted by classes on "the theology and practice of prayer"; some developed in seminar groups on evangelism. Out of the latter came ventures in Christian witness which are still bearing fruit today.

When I began my work in missionary radio with the broadcast WORDS OF HOPE, I was no longer a pastor of a congregation or a member in a closely knit seminary community. I felt more keenly than ever the need for Christian fellowship and small group interaction. I decided to "issue a call."

I told several friends in my home congregation what I was looking for. I wanted to be a part of a group that would meet weekly to pray—with a special focus. We would begin with a passage of Scripture. We would share our needs and burdens, struggles and sorrows, hopes, and dreams. We would pray for one another, for our families, and for those within our congregation. But we wouldn't stop there. We would go on to the wider concerns of God's kingdom. We would pray for the renewal of the church and the spread of the gospel in every land. We would intercede for warring nations and suffering peoples.

Some whom I invited liked the idea but didn't feel able to invest the time. Others simply declined. Two or three came occasionally, but didn't commit themselves to the group. Some who began with us have since moved away. A nucleus of six remains, four of whom have been together for over ten years. It would be hard for me now to think about life without that group. So many experiences shared, so many prayers offered, so much freedom enjoyed to be ourselves and open our hearts! What a gift—to pray with friends!

I had a concern for another group outside our congregation, a group to focus on the concerns of our city, our local institutions, and the church at large. Again, not everyone invited was able to take part. But a few from Hope College and Western Seminary, from the business community and the pastorate banded together for weekly prayer. That group too has continued for over ten years. The bonds between us are close, and the shared vision has enlarged. For these partners, too, in the life of prayer, I will always be grateful. When I considered some years ago a major career move and totted up good reasons for staying where I was, these small groups with their large prayers were at the top of my list.

Sometimes Helen and I have issued a call together. Four of us couples used to meet to share our struggles and find mutual support. There was always a prayer together to crown the evening. Another group was called together for Bible study, with the special aim of inviting nonchurched friends to join us from time to time. There, too, we tried to wrestle with what we found in Scripture and bring it before God in our prayers.

Still another group—the longest enduring of all—has a different format. For over fifteen years we've called it "fun night." The fun is all in being together. The dinner, the ritual, the ridiculous games—all of that is simply the setting for an always-fresh experience of shared laughter.

The lightheartedness is never trivial. The families involved—all of us—have gone through great pain. We recognize the fun as a priceless healing gift. We see it as a celebration of life in the midst of sorrow and death. It is an offering of love we present to each other. The clue to its real meaning always appears in the moments of prayer around the dinner table. Together we are—with the Joy Giver always in the midst.

Sometimes you have a friend with whom you discover a shared vision. You find that you feel the same need, the same heart hunger. You help each other to articulate that and realize in a moment of common insight that it's what you both have been searching for. Then you send forth a call together.

My friend and I did that only a few months ago. We wanted to be in a group that talks about books, that stimulates and stretches the mind. But we wanted also to turn what we learn into prayer, to see every discipline in the light of God's kingdom.

We thought about whom we would like to invite—people of several ages, from varied disciplines, all intellectually curious, all seeking to be Christian, but delightfully different. We told them about the group, one at a time, and asked them if they would be interested. This time we "batted a thousand!" Each one "wanted in." Now we look forward to those meetings for weeks in advance. No one wants to miss what the others have to offer. We read, raise questions, discuss, debate, and then pray. All we consider, we spread before God. "More light, Lord!"

What about you? Is there something you would like to share with others and mix with prayer? Issue a call. Ask for wisdom about whom to invite. Think of the most likely candidate—the one with whom you most sense a kindred spirit. Ask her first, or him. Tell that person what you are needing and seeking. Maybe she or he can help clarify the vision, or suggest other names.

When some invited ones decline, it may seem like a personal rejection. It probably won't be. Your call puts no one under obligation. It leaves them free, and that's how you want them to feel. But God usually has someone prepared to answer a call like that. It's worth the risk. What you call into being may mean more than you dream, to you, your group, and God's coming kingdom.

For Response and Resolve

Believing that God delights in the united prayers of his people, let me call others to join me in prayer and be ready to heed their calls to me.

For Reading and Meditation

Psalm 34:1–3
Matthew 18:19, 20
Acts 1:12–14; 2:42–47; 4:23–31; 6:1–7; 12:12; 13:1–3;
    14:23; 16:25; 20:36; 21:5
James 5:13–16

For Reflection and Discussion

1. In what sense should we "shut the door" and "pray to our Father in secret"?

2. Identify several instances in the Book of Acts of the early Christians praying together.
3. What is the significance of "agreeing" or "harmonizing" with one another in our petitions?
4. What kind of call to united prayer are you responding to now? What kind of call can you send forth?

15

You Can Shape the Future

*And another angel came and stood at the altar
with a golden censer; and he was given much
incense to mingle with the prayers of all the saints
upon the golden altar before the throne; and the
smoke of the incense rose with the prayers of the
saints from the hand of the angel before God.
Then the angel took the censer and filled it with
fire from the altar and threw it on the earth; and
there were peals of thunder, loud noises, flashes
of lightning, and an earthquake (Rev. 8:3–5).*

*Prayer is the most intimate and effective form
of Christian action. All other work comes far
behind, and it is Christian work, active Christian
righteousness, the doing of the will of God . . . only
to the extent that it derives from prayer.*

Karl Barth

*What matters is the sheer existence of those who
pray. It is not without significance for a people
that there should be in it a little band of those who
bear up the whole nation vicariously in their
prayers.*

Helmut Thielicke

Some time ago I was privileged to attend a "confer-
ence on the future." A number of churchmen gathered in
Atlanta, Georgia, seeking to anticipate what may lie
ahead in the final years of this century and especially to

169

plan for future Christian witness. Experts in various fields gave us their projections about what to expect. At the close of the meeting, we gathered in small groups to draw up our own imagined scenarios of coming events. It was a fascinating, mind-stretching experience.

We happened to meet in a hotel undergoing extensive renovations. In many parts of the building, we saw scaffolding, movable partitions, canvas draped over this and that. The management was trying to make the best of a somewhat embarrassing situation. A number of humorous, half-apologetic signs had been posted in the lobby and on the walls of the elevators. One pleaded directly: PARDON OUR MESS. Another said, DON'T KNOCK THIS PROJECT; THE CONTRACTOR MAY BE STANDING RIGHT BESIDE YOU. One in particular I remember noticing several times: WHEN THE DUST SETTLES, YOU'RE GOING TO SEE ONE GORGEOUS HOTEL.

When the scaffolding would at last be taken down and the partitions removed, the drapes drawn back and everything tidied up, then, we were told, the true beauty of the hotel would appear. Incidentally, I've been back there since and the prophecy has been duly fulfilled!

That's a parable of what I want to think about now: the lasting behind the temporary; the glorious behind the cluttered; the real behind the merely apparent. If there's one book in all the world that gives us that perspective, it is the last book of the Bible, the Revelation that God gave to Jesus, which he sent and signified by his servant John. There we see beyond the appearances, behind the facades, to the way things *are.*

Think, for example, about Jesus of Nazareth. Who is he, really? Many people in the world of his time, first-century Rome, had never heard of him. To some who had, he was simply a wandering teacher in an outlying province of the empire. He was said to have done remarkable things, but his movement had been easily put down by the authorities. The man held no lands, commanded no fighting men, wrote no books, and at the end was cut off in his prime. When Roman soldiers came to arrest him, even his closest followers had fled in panic. On trial, he had come up with nothing to say in his own defense. When finally executed, he had lasted only a few hours on the cross.

There was a rumor, of course, that he had been raised from the dead. But only a group of his unlettered friends claimed to have seen him. Skeptics could argue that there was no official notice of such an event, and no proof. To most of those people (and to millions today), Jesus has been only a name, a shadowy figure around whom legend and superstition have gathered. He is Swinburne's "pale Galilean," a comforting memory, perhaps, to little children and to the elderly, but of no real significance to hard-driving people in our complex, changing world.

In the Book of the Revelation, we see him differently. On the Isle of Patmos, John encountered Jesus as the risen One. His feet were like burnished bronze, his eyes a flame of fire. His countenance was like the sun shining in full strength. He had the stars in his hands and his voice was like the sound of a thousand Niagaras. When John saw him, he fell down at his feet as one dead. But Jesus laid his right hand on him and said, "Fear not, I am the first and the last, and the living one; I died, and behold, I am alive forevermore, and I have the keys of Death and Hades" (Rev. 1:18). King of kings and Lord of lords—that's who Jesus is!

What about history—what meaning does it have for modern man? Many people see it as nothing more than a chance sequence of events. In Shakespeare's words, it is "a tale told by an idiot, full of sound and fury, signifying nothing" (*Macbeth*). All of us are the "poor players" who "strut and fret" for a brief hour on the stage and then disappear.

Others see history as an endless cycle, a carousel of returning ages. The seasons and the colors change, but everything comes around again. There's no ultimate meaning, no final goal. For still others, history is a monument to man's greatness, a record of his colossal achievements. "Glory to man in the highest," they sing, "for man is the measure of things."

But in the Revelation, we see history in a different light. John writes:

> After this I looked, and lo, in heaven an open door! And the first voice, which I had heard speaking to me like a trumpet, said, "Come up hither, and I will show you what must take place..." and lo, a throne stood in heaven... and round the throne was a rainbow... (4:1–3). And I saw in the right hand of him who was seated on the throne a scroll written within and on the back, sealed with seven seals; and I saw a strong angel proclaiming with a loud voice, "Who is worthy to open the scroll and break its seals?" And no one in heaven or on earth or under the earth was able to open the scroll or to look into it, and I wept much that no one was found worthy to open the scroll or to look into it. Then one of the elders said to me, "Weep not; lo, the Lion of the tribe of Judah, the Root of David, has conquered, so that he can open the scroll and its seven seals" (5:1–5).
>
> ...And I saw a Lamb standing, as though it had been slain...and he went and took the scroll from the right hand of him who was seated on the throne... and they sang a new song, saying,
> > "Worthy art thou to take the scroll
> >   and to open its seals,
> >   for thou wast slain and by thy blood
> >   didst ransom men for God
> >   from every tribe and tongue and
> >   people and nation...."
> "Worthy is the Lamb who was slain!..." (vv. 6, 7, 9, 12).

That scroll is the book of destiny, the secret purpose of almighty God. As the Lamb takes the scroll and opens its

seals, all the events of history gradually unfold themselves. History is really *his* story, his track through time.
The Lamb at the throne of God is the Lord to whom
authority belongs. He is the Initiator, the prime Mover in
this world. The headlines and the history books all point
beyond themselves to the mystery of his sovereign work.
That's what the drama of the ages is principally about.

Now for one more scene. We find this in Revelation,
chapter 8. John sees an angel standing by the golden
altar before the throne. He is given much incense which
he mingles together with the prayers of all the saints, and
offers on the golden altar. As the fragrance rises before
the throne, the angel takes the censer, scoops from the
altar fire, and hurls a shower of coals on the earth. At that
moment, there are peals of thunder, voices in tumult,
lightning flashes, and a fearsome earthquake (8:1–5).

What does this mysterious vision mean? It discloses
the moving forces behind world events. What are the
inner dynamics that make things happen? What are
the forces that relentlessly shape the future? They are
the prayers of the saints and the heavenly fire. Above the
arms races and political intrigues, behind economic di-
sasters or movements of reform, the risen Christ is opening the seals of the book, working out his strange design
through the burning petitions of his people.

"But," someone objects, "aren't the true movers of
history the oil barons, the political strongmen, the mo-
guls of the mass media, the heads of multinational corpo-
rations?" Yes, they have their role to play, but mightier
than all of them are the prayers of the saints and the fire
of God.

It's good to know that. The powers and pressures of
this age are all too real. We must face them constantly.
But we can rejoice that they are less than ultimate. The
fiercest of them are like lions on the Lord's leash. He says
to them, as to the proud waves of the sea, "Thus far, and

no farther." And, at the last, the lives and prayers of faithful men and women prove mightier by far.

I hope that many of you, reading these words now, will be activists in this world, that you will hold office, exert influence, shape policy. I hope that you will write books, discover cures, launch crusades. I hope that you will struggle for justice and freedom, that you will give yourself to combat racism and poverty and war, and that in all things you will hold forth the gospel of the risen Christ.

But I hope that you won't be barren activists, quickly losing enthusiasm, becoming manipulative or discouraged because everyone doesn't rally to your cause. I hope you won't be numbered among those soon-weary activists who are spurred on by fragile ideals and depend on their own meager resources.

Prayer, real prayer, is not a substitute for action, not a pious retreat from the world. It doesn't take the place, surely, of costly involvement. It is rather the *prerequisite* for all action, all involvement that will prove significant, fruitful, and lasting.

Theologian P.T. Forsyth has put it like this: "Prayer is for the religious life what original research is for science. By it we get direct contact with reality." In this case the "real" is the risen Lord, who is opening the seals of the book. Prayer is our acknowledgment that the promised future comes "not by might, nor by power, but by [God's] Spirit" (Zech. 4:6). It's the expression of our dependence, the confession that the kingdom and the power and the glory belong to him. In prayer, we say with Judah's beleaguered king, "...We are powerless against this great multitude that is coming against us. We do not know what to do, but our eyes are upon thee" (2 Chron. 20:12).

There are Christians in the world today who are awakening to the reality of these things, who are beginning to give to prayer a more central and dominant place in their lives than ever before. There are groups springing up here and there in which people gather not only to listen to God's Word, to share their joys and struggles, to pray for one another and their loved ones—but to go beyond that. They pray for large concerns of God's kingdom; for some peaceful solution to the tragic hostilities of the Middle East, of northern Ireland, of El Salvador, and Nicaragua. They cry out for a great breakthrough of the Christian gospel in the Muslim world; for a mighty awakening in the stagnant churches of Western Europe; for multitudes of the world's hungry to be provided for; for a purifying tide of revival to sweep through our decaying cultures; for the earth to be filled with the knowledge of God's glory as the waters cover the sea.

This has always been God's way, to prepare for world-transforming movements by calling his people to earnest prayer. Remember the believers in Antioch, waiting on God, worshiping, praying, fasting? The Holy Spirit said, "Set apart for me Barnabas and Saul for the work to which I have called them" (Acts 13:2). Then, from the midst of that prayer gathering, the gospel spread like a prairie fire through Asia Minor and Europe.

If we could see what goes on behind the scenes today, how many dynamic movements have been begun and carried forward through little groups of believers at prayer, we would adopt a different view about the things that matter in this world and the forces that rule. May I challenge you to join yourself to a band like that—a future-shaping fellowship? Or, if you don't know of such a group, will you call one into being? Speak to a few friends of like mind. Ask God's Spirit to direct you into what faith dares to call "world-transforming prayer."

Of one thing the Word makes us sure: when the scaffolding has been taken down and the partitions removed, when the drapes are drawn back, and the glory of the Lord appears, we will discover that more than any of us dared to hope was accomplished here—through our prayers and heaven's fire.

You can do it, friends. You can welcome the gift and pursue the calling. You can give yourself to a lifetime of prayer. And though no one may ever know of your labor or connect it with your name, your prayers can make an enormous difference. Dare to believe that. Dare to venture on it. You can shape the future after God's design. You can pray!

For Response and Resolve

Because the shaping forces in world history are the prayers of the saints and the heavenly fire, let me serve God and my generation through a lifetime of believing prayer.

For Reading and Meditation

Mark 11:20–24
Acts 16:25–34
James 5:16–18
Revelation 8:1–5